TEACHING
WRITING
WITH COMPUTERS

TEACHING
WRITING
WITH COMPUTERS
The POWER Process

Gwen Solomon

Prentice-Hall Inc., Englewood Cliffs, New Jersey 07632

Library of Congress Cataloging in Publication Data

Solomon, Gwen, (date)
  Teaching writing with computers.

    Includes index.
    1. English language—Composition and exercises—
Study and teaching—Data processing. 2. Computer-
assisted instruction. 3. Word processing. I. Title.
PE1404.S65 1986   808'.042'07   85-3471
ISBN 0-13-896366-5
ISBN 0-13-896358-4 (pbk.)

        Editorial/production supervision and
          interior design: Shirley Stern
        Cover photo: Ken Karp
        Manufacturing buyer: Barbara Kittle
        Cover design: Bruce Kenselaar

© 1986 by Gwen Solomon

Printed in the United States of America

10 9 8 7 6 5 4 3 2 1

ISBN 0-13-896366-5 {01}

ISBN 0-13-896358-4 {01} {pbk}

PRENTICE-HALL INTERNATIONAL (UK) LIMITED, *London*
PRENTICE-HALL of AUSTRALIA PTY. LIMITED, *Sydney*
EDITORA PRENTICE-HALL DO BRASIL, LTDA., *Rio de Janeiro*
PRENTICE-HALL CANADA INC., *Toronto*
PRENTICE-HALL HISPONOAMERICANA, S.A., *Mexico*
PRENTICE-HALL OF INDIA PRIVATE LIMITED, *New Delhi*
PRENTICE-HALL OF JAPAN, INC., *Tokyo*
PRENTICE-HALL OF SOUTHEAST ASIA PTE. LTD., *Singapore*
WHITEHALL BOOKS LIMITED, *Wellington, New Zealand*

To my husband Stan for his assistance,
to my daughter Debbie for her patience,
and to my parents, Helen and Richard Wolff,
for a lifetime of encouragement and support.

Contents

Preface

There is a conspiracy about computer use in the schools. The technical people who first discovered this machine knew they had a good thing, so they used a highly specialized vocabulary and even created new languages to frighten us off. We fell for the trick, too. Many Language Arts people were reluctant to acknowledge the new technology, let alone use computers.

But some of us uncovered the conspiracy. We investigated, and saw that the computer is merely a tool and that one of its best uses is to process words. That's our field, folks. We're the people who use words, who play with them, who teach a love of them to children.

This book was written to break up the conspiracy. When all Language Arts people know that these machines are really for us, we'll get them out of the mathematics laboratories and into the rest of the school. We'll share what we know—that writing with a word processor can improve children's abilities to think and to communicate. Then teachers in all subject areas will have their students writing. I propose a new conspiracy. Let's prove to everyone else what we've known all along: that writing is the most important subject in the curriculum.

TEACHING
WRITING
WITH COMPUTERS

Chapter 1

The POWER Process

"Who me? Write? What do I say? How should I say it? Who wants to read it anyway?" Sound familiar? Many of your students and mine experience a fear of writing. Yet they can overcome their fears and improve their writing easily. At last we have a tool that will help them.

We can use word processing, one of the applications of computer technology, to help our students. After all, students write for a living, so to speak, and must learn to write effectively. Word processing can make a difference. So, too, can the method of writing that students practice. The process proposed here involves power: the power of the human mind, the power of the written word, and the power of the computer. These can be combined to help students learn to communicate well.

THE POWER PROCESS

The POWER Process is a learning process. Because word processing makes writing, revising, and reading the work almost painless, for a student who uses a word processor the process of rewriting becomes second nature. Students internalize the process, making it their own, and thereby learn how to write well; the teacher acts as a guide and as a consultant.

POWER is an acronym for the five steps involved in the process I want to propose:

Prewrite
Organize
Write
Exchange
Revise

Let's see what each of these steps involves.

PREWRITING

Prewriting is guided discovery. It can involve a discussion about a topic or an exploration of a technique or a way of looking at something. Students can work individually, in small groups, or as a class. You can pose a serious philosophical issue, raise a question that relates to students' lives or classwork, or use a gimmick. Through the discussion or exercise, you lead your students to focus on an issue or on a concept. Thus you help them assemble their ideas before they decide how to organize them or write them down.

ORGANIZING

Organizing involves taking the topic, technique, or perception and formulating a central focus for writing. This step can be informal (involving no more than jotting notes about theme, character, and plot) or formal (involving the complete outlining of an essay). Actually, the step entails focusing on the ideas assembled in the prewriting stage until a sensible arrangement of those ideas suggests itself. Students can work first individually and then in pairs or groups to refine their ideas.

Traditionally, after a writing assignment is given and explained, students are required to work alone to write their material. They hand in a finished essay and you return it for possible rewriting with a few comments (and a grade). Essentially, they are working in a vacuum. They have no idea whether they have approached the topic in the most intelligent or creative way possible. They lack the advantage of knowing what others are thinking or doing. Until the work has been handed in and returned, there is no feedback.

Both the prewriting discussion and the group assistance in organizing, that characterize the POWER method, can help eliminate the fear of writing that comes from working alone.

WRITING

Writing involves taking the ideas that have just been organized and expressing them on a screen, then printing out the words onto paper. Because of the capabilities of the word processor, the student's words are not "carved in stone." They can and will be changed. Students can type their text as quickly as the ideas flow; errors in sequencing, mechanics, and form can be fixed later. Students can write and fix obvious errors as they work, or just write as much as possible and then go back to see what corrections they want to make.

Not even a professional writer can create polished work at one sitting. It is impossible to generate ideas, refine them, and edit for mechanical errors without respite. If students write and then have time to think about and go over their work, the final product will be superior. With a word processor, rough drafts become final drafts without any need for the student to copy over what was good to begin with.

EXCHANGING

Exchanging involves presenting the written ideas to a peer editorial group for analysis, discussion, and help. Through this process students become aware of the reactions of others and can experience the impact of their own words. Questions such as What is your point? What evidence do you give? Why does your character show that emotion? What does this word mean? are the sort that students should ask of each other in their groups. If even one member of the group is unable to understand something or follow the writer's logic, the group should ask for clarification. It is easier to spot errors of all varieties (logic, detail, proof, or mechanics) in others' work than in one's own. After all, the writer obviously knows what he or she meant, but that the readers will understand as well does not necessarily follow.

Through this process of exchanging, students learn to say what they mean. They accept peer review because it is a cooperative effort; they are all dependent on the others in the group to help them produce the best work that they can. Students are not reluctant to take or discuss the group's advice because, with a word processor, they can easily change any passage that doesn't work in their text.

With a word processor students can print out multiple copies of their work, and each member of the group can have a copy to read and to scribble notes on. Without such copies, when a student (or the teacher) reads aloud, the others often lose track of what is said, what questions they have, and what comments they want to make. With a copy for individual reading and use, students can provide real help to each other.

REVISING

Revising is a system of making changes. Students can print out what they have written and take a copy home to read. New ideas, better ways of expressing ideas, and better use of language will occur to them. Changes can be made on the rough copy and entered on the screen during the next session. In addition, during the revising stage students take the help given in the exchange procedure and apply it to the text on the screen. Each student makes changes in form, content, and manner of expression and prints out another copy. He or she can return to the exchange procedure for more help and then revise some more. Revision includes editing for mechanical errors but is not limited to this. Words, sentences, and even ideas can easily be removed, rearranged, and replaced with a word processor. When the entire process is complete—that is, when the student is satisfied that his or her best effort is on the printed page—the essay is finished. The student can hand it in with confidence.

THE TEACHER'S ROLE

Your role as the teacher in each stage is to guide and help individuals and groups. The prewriting activity is usually a whole-class session in which you guide students to the point where they can begin work. During the other stages, you work with individual students and groups to suggest methods of handling topics and to provide feedback about the ideas under discussion. Thus students know what your perspective is. Again, they are not working in isolation.

The last step for the teacher is, as always, to grade the papers. If your students have used word processors, the task will be easier than it was when they wrote in the traditional way. To begin with, word-processed papers are always legible, and students can be instructed to set a margin wide enough for your comments. In addition, students who have used word processors will have done true revising, so their work will be superior to their previous efforts. As the students internalize the process of writing and revising, you will be able to make more sophisticated and valuable comments.

In addition, you can monitor student improvement by requesting printouts of drafts during the writing and revising stages. You can also see long-term changes in student work by calling up various papers. Theme 4 should be better than Theme 1. If it is not, you and the student together can analyze his or her problems and decide on a strategy for improvement.

This combination of word processing and the POWER Process is an effective way for you to help students learn.

Chapter 2
What Is Word Processing?

Word processing—what a funny name. It sounds like something you do in one of those fancy blenders. Just what is word processing, anyway?

ADVANTAGES OF WORD PROCESSING

Let's start with an analogy. Once upon a time, we travelled on horses; later we began to transport ourselves on bicycles, then in cars. They all do the same thing—provide transportation. But I wouldn't take the family across the country on horseback (or on a bike either). While all three methods of transport serve the same purpose, the style, the comfort, and the quality of the trip differ considerably depending on which method you choose.

The same is true of writing. The pen, the pencil, and the typewriter do the same thing as a word processor—get our ideas down in front of us. But the style, the comfort, and the quality of the trip. . .

Now for a definition. Word processing is a method of typing any text and revising and editing easily. A special program, called word-processing software, tells the computer how to do what you want with your words.

Sounds complicated? Well, let's go back to our fancy blender (or food processor). You take chunks of food, insert them, mix them up, and voilà—instant pâté or some such delicacy. With a word processor, you type your words using the computer keyboard, insert and delete words, mix them around, and voilà—a finished product: your novel, poem, or friendly letter. You can watch your ingredients moving around in a Cuisinart, and you can see your words appear on the computer monitor. You remove your pâté to serve it on Delft china, and you tell your printer to deliver your essay in perfect form on computer paper. This is really where the analogy ends. If your pâté doesn't quite hit the mark, there's nothing you can do.

But if your perfect copy is not quite as good as you thought, you can simply rearrange things once again on the computer screen and print out another perfect copy.

Even though we should be talking about students, they can wait a bit. You are the writer who's most important right now. At least for me it worked this way. While I was using drill-and-practice programs on the computers in class, I spent my own computer time word processing. I fell in love with the word processor on my own account first and realized what my students could get out of it later. So let's talk about word processing in relation to us.

HOW WORD PROCESSING WORKS

How are words processed? We'll start with the equipment, or hardware. This isn't a book on how to operate computers, so I'll make the explanation brief. To do word processing, you need a computer, a disk drive, a monitor, and a printer (with cables to connect the various components). Then you need software, a word-processing program. You'll also want blank disks on which to store what you write and paper for the printer.

Let's put ourselves in front of all of this equipment and start from the beginning. First, turn on everything that has a switch. Now insert the disk that contains the word-processing program into the disk drive and load the program into the computer's memory. A message on the screen will tell when that's done. Now remove that disk and insert your file disk into the drive. (Please use an initialized disk—one that has been set up to take information from your computer.)

Your monitor probably shows a basically clean screen. (Some programs give you help at the top or on an instruction screen.) Use the keyboard to type in whatever you want to say, and use the special functions of the software to make what you have typed look the way you want. Add a word here; take out a phrase there; move a sentence from one place to another, for example. Then save the text on your file disk and use the print options to design your printed page. Print out what you have written, and you're in business.

That's it. Any future changes are made in the same fashion: Load your text into the computer the next day, week, or month; revise and edit on the screen; save the improved text; and print out a new copy.

You're probably asking, "What happens to my words?" To be brief, the computer recognizes the electronic impulses you send when you press the keys. The software (word-processing program) tells the computer to manipulate these impulses so that your instructions are followed. You press letter keys and they appear on the screen as words. You press a special function key or a control-key sequence, and things happen to your words.

Professional writers who try using word processors seldom go back to typewriters, just as those who tried electric typewriters a decade or two ago almost never returned to manuals. The most efficient tool is the best. It will take a little time and effort to learn the procedures your word-processing software requires to do the things you want, but the effort is worth your while. The benefits of replacing the typewriter with the word processor are phenomenal.

THE KEYBOARD

Let's look at the keyboard for a minute. Both typewriters and word processors use the traditional QWERTY keyboard (named for the top row of letters), but on a word processor, you get a few extras. Think about the carriage return, for example. Electric typewriters are physically easier to use than manual typewriters: You can press a button when you want to start a new line, instead of raising your arm and shoving the carriage back with a lever. But—and this is a big *but*—at the end of a typed line, you still must stop to make a decision. Will your word fit? Should you hyphenate? Will you press *margin release* and let the word hang over?

The Return Feature

Well, that time-consuming nonsense is in the past. The RETURN key on a word processor allows you to move to the next line when you want to (for poetry formats or to start a new paragraph), but for typing line after line, there is no carriage return. Your words simply move to the next line if they don't fit on the first. This is called *word wraparound*. It speeds up your typing (Pavlov would cry: you never respond to the sound of a bell.) and allows you to concentrate on your ideas, not on your page.

The Insert Feature

Since no one writes perfect copy the first time, many of the features of a word processor have to do with fixing mistakes. With the INSERT feature, for example, you can put the "e" back into "computer" when you've typed "computr." Or you can insert a sentence or even a whole paragraph into the middle of your work when you're at the end of it. For example, I wrote this paragraph after I read the original text and saw I hadn't explained enough.

The Delete Feature

With the DELETE function, you can turn "compouter" into "computer." This makes you like Letterman from *Sesame Street*, able to turn words that grate into words that are great. You can hide those typos, misspellings, and illogical thoughts so no one will ever see them. (Does she or doesn't she? Only her computer knows for sure.) No one would imagine the mistakes I made in this book—luckily— because I've banished all the evidence.

Block Moves

Another handy feature, called BLOCK MOVES, helps you rearrange your ideas. If I had written this paragraph after the next one and wanted to exchange them or even put them into a different book, I could instruct my computer to do either. My wish is its command.

The Merge Feature

Word processing lets you put various things together that you originally thought were separate topics. Each chapter of this book was written as an individual entity and joined with the others later by means of a feature called MERGE.

Formatting

Have you noticed that each chapter heading is centered perfcctly on the page? I could never get the knack of that on a typewriter (something about counting by 2's, I think). Now I can tell my word processor, "Center that line!" I don't really yell; I just press the right keys, and the job will be done. This is an example of formatting, or giving instructions about how my printed page will look. Other features enable me to indent, tabulate (something else that was beyond me on a typewriter), and underline.

Search and Replace

There are more word-processing capabilities, too. You can be Sherlock Holmes and SEARCH for a word or expression that you know you used somewhere when you can't remember in what context. In fact, you can find every occurrence of the word; your word processor will do the walking. It can even REPLACE that word with another in as many places as you want. This feature is handy when you have to write the expression "word processor" about a million times (as in this book). You can type "WP" and later instantly replace these initials with the correct phrase throughout the manuscript. There are more features available, too, but I haven't needed them myself, so I'm not including them. You can read the manual that came with your program to see what other tricks it will do.

FASTER WRITING ON A WORD PROCESSOR

Now a word about speed. When you don't worry about making typing errors, you type faster. When you type faster, your ideas can be put down faster. When you put your ideas down faster, you have time to come up with additional ideas. When you have additional ideas, you type more. When you type more, you can write more than anyone ever wanted to know about whatever (about word processing, for instance, as I am doing now) and get rid of the unnecessary details later.

By the way, did you ever forget where you were and want to see what you had just typed? Lift that paper bale, peer over the roller, hold up the sheet of paper. The next thing you know, you've forgotten why you wanted to read that sentence or what you want to say next. On a word processor, about a page of text is visible on the screen in front of you. And you don't have to shuffle papers to find the previous page. You can SCROLL—move around in your text—at the flick of a keystroke.

MAKING CORRECTIONS

I always seem to find typos after I've removed the paper from the typewriter. Now, I know that there are people adept at reinserting the page and lining up the type just right so they can use Wite-Out or Ko-Rec-Type to fix the error. I can't. Now I don't have to. I fix the typo on the screen and print out another copy. In fact, fixing typos is an ongoing process. Typos multiply; there always seem to be more. And when you discover "the the" in your text, Wite-Out won't help. If you tried to paint over the mistake, you'd have a blotch on your page and would have to retype the whole thing anyway. Word processing to the rescue: Remove the offending word (even sentences or paragraphs that you've changed your mind about) and print out another copy. Never retype anything that was correct to start with; simply fix what you want to change.

What does all of this mean? Well, believe it or not, convenience releases creativity. When you don't have to worry about the mechanics of your writing, you can be spontaneous in the creation of ideas. You can write ideas in any order and move them into a more logical sequence later. You can write in a stream-of-consciousness style and insert punctuation later. You can get ideas down before you forget them, and make them look pretty later. You can even write your first book (as I did). I never would have attempted this book without a word processor.

What happens when you use a word processor is that revision becomes a natural part of the process of composition. You write ideas and revise them later. You think about them some more and then revise again. You can work on hard copy or directly on the screen. There is no more retyping of drafts; you just keep fixing the first draft until it is the way you want it; then you print out a final draft. You know that your work will look perfect, so you concentrate on making it sould perfect too.

Chapter 3
Processing Ideas

"I have a good idea," I said. And that was how it all began. I was at a meeting in the principal's office when I uttered those memorable first words. "I'd like to use computers in my English classes." I had just been introduced to the fascinating world of computers and programming, and I wanted to get my hands on my very own computers for my students. Of course, I wasn't sure exactly how I'd use them, but uncertainty never stopped me from opening my mouth.

PROJECT ETC.

Through blind good luck, my principal was able to tap some of those year-end "use or lose" funds, and we were in business. In the fall of 1983, with 16 student stations, a network (a system to link the computers), a host computer, a printer, and very little software, I began. I called my plan PROJECT ETC.–English Through Computers. That made it sound more formal, not like a one-person operation, but like a real educational program for the eighties.

The First Attempt

I couldn't teach programming; that was done in the mathematics department. But computers were a natural for individualized instruction, weren't they? From the beginning, the students were captivated by the machines. They finally had control over something technical in the world. They learned how to use equipment few others in the school could fathom and felt a sense of achievement. They loved playing word games, alphabetizing lists, reading cloze exercises, and punctuating sentences. But their reading didn't improve any more than it had using other methods; nor did their writing or thinking skills grow. So what were they learning? Sure, they put up with drill-and-practice routines on the computer when they had rejected the same type of work in workbooks. Sure, the software was patient, reinforcing, persistent. But something was missing.

A Better Approach

Not quite sure why my computers weren't the miracles I had expected, I decided to try another approach. I had been using word-processing software for my own writing and knew that this was the way of my future. So I offered my students the chance to write by computer as well. To make this way of writing sound special, I called it the POWER Process, but the method really developed simply because I changed my own way of writing when I got a word processor. My method became a mixture of things I had always done and new techniques that were possible because of the equipment. This combination is what I offered my students.

THE STAGES OF COMPOSITION

Making Notes

To begin with, I can't think without a pencil in my hand. I used to handwrite everything (in pencil, so I could erase). I never learned to think at the typewriter because I was so concerned about making mistakes that I couldn't be creative. So I wrote in longhand and typed only my final draft. Now I use a word processor to write, but I still grab a pencil to jot down notes first. My way of absorbing and using information has always been to begin by scribbling notes about what I plan to do. When I have these notes in front of me, I'm able to start writing on the processor more easily and to continue in a logical way. Then I reread, think about what I've written, and revise. I encouraged my students to use this method because I believed that if word processing made the process so much easier for me, it could work for them too.

My first step is to write down whatever ideas on the topic come into my head. That's my prewriting. In the classroom, I start a prewriting discussion or use an exercise to get the students to consider an idea. Sometimes they work alone and then talk about what they've come up with; sometimes they work in pairs, in groups, or as an entire class to brainstorm.

Organizing Thoughts

My second step is to organize my notes into what I think I want to say. Sometimes I'll talk to someone about my ideas; sometimes I'll just let the ideas float around in my head for a while. With or without someone else's opinion, I always have something thoughtful to bring to the computer, something that helps me start writing. After my students have been working with an idea, I have them organize their thinking in terms of a specific issue they want to pursue. Sometimes they produce brief notes; sometimes they need to create a structured outline.

Writing a First Draft

Eventually, I sit down at the word processor and write. I always come up with more ideas as I type. In fact, I write the way I talk, meandering; so my ideas are rarely in order when I'm finished. That doesn't matter anymore, thanks to the computer. I save and print out whatever I've typed and put the draft aside. My students also know that they don't have to produce polished copy immediately; they use their notes and write rough drafts.

Rereading, Reviewing, Reconsidering

After a respite from my work, I read over the printout. New ideas and a better order occur to me, so I make notes in the margin and then go back to the computer. In my old, longhand days, it was often difficult to read the corrections, and once something had been typed, it was finished. It might have been painted with a pint of Wite-Out, but I wouldn't undertake extensive revisions for fear of retyping. Now I call up my text and revise it until it says what I want to say in the way I want to say it. Usually I have to revise and print out several times before I'm satisfied with my product. What freedom to know I can keep playing with an essay and not worry about the paper!

My students have an extra advantage: each other. Rarely can an adult find someone to read what he or she has written. When I do twist someone's arm, I find that another's perspective helps me refine my thinking. That's why the exchange procedure is so important for students' writing. They use each other's insights to improve their work. Then they can revise purposefully.

Revising

I have my students go through numerous readings and revisions, but there is really a limit to how well a student can perceive differences in successive drafts of his or her own work. Again, here's where the exchange procedure works. The students revise and then consult with each other again before they revise even more. The quality of their thinking improves when they discuss the logic of their ideas and their use of detail with fellow students. They begin to know what is expected of them and to express their thoughts clearly. Thus the quality of their writing improves as well.

SUCCESS OF THE POWER PROCESS

Because the word processor freed them from the tedious aspects of writing and revising, my students were able to adopt my five-step approach to writing. They discovered that they could improve not only the final product but also the way in which they dealt with information. When writing topics came from other subject areas, they developed a perspective that made the topics relevant. Information was no longer a series of unrelated facts but became the basis for thematic thinking and writing.

Even at the beginning, my students were eager to use the word processors, eager to print out their work and share it with others. For the first time, they were willing to think about what they were doing. They wrote, carefully rereading their work and revising, not just fixing up the mechanical errors I had marked. They were willing to consider what they had written and how to improve it. My bulletin boards and walls were soon covered with student efforts. The pride that writing now engendered was incredible.

SPECIAL TEACHING TECHNIQUES

The POWER Process worked not only with my creative writing class but also with the Basic Skills classes. We started with poetry in all classes for two reasons. First, I found that students were willing to write brief passages and then play with formatting their words into poetic form on the screen. Second, it was easier for the students to see the process in action with only short lines to consider.

I found certain writing techniques that are hard to teach in a traditional classroom easier to teach with a word processor and easier for students to understand and practice as well. For example, most of my students did not offer enough detail in their writing. So we tried an expansion exercise. We took a general term, *girl*, and expanded it on the screen by adding specific qualifications: "small girl in white dress." Students were then able to write detailed phrases, such as "a pigtailed two-year-old in a white-eyelet pinafore standing in a field," by inserting, deleting, and moving words. The students' use of detail improved tremendously.

We talked about abstract ideas for a while as a prewriting activity, and discovered how concrete images convey the feelings of those ideas. We played with images, creating them, arranging them, expanding them. And we created a mini-magazine, COMPUTER POETRY. All of my classes—honor students, creative writers, and students whose skills were below grade level—contributed equally and equally well. All were so excited by the possibility of publication that they worked hard to produce poems of quality. After all, everyone would read what they had written when we published in June.

Over the course of the following year, I tried many different techniques for various forms of writing practice. Some worked well; others did not. Using word processors to teach writing is an ongoing learning situation both for me and for my students. What I share in this book is what has worked so far. As you use these techniques and ideas, you will refine them even more and find others that work in your classroom. As our students learn, so do we. That is the nature of education; it is always fluid.

Chapter 4
Classroom Writing

A major problem in teaching writing is the blank-paper phenomenon. A clean, crisp sheet of paper causes panic because it means that students must commit themselves for posterity. After all, what idea is worthy of indelible ink? Many students are overwhelmed before they begin because they don't realize that they have good ideas. The result is blank stares at the blank page or false starts and crumpled papers. With word processing, students have no paper to crumple, but there is still a blank screen waiting for their imprint, which could be a formidable obstacle. Therefore, we have to begin by reducing the stress so students can write.

UNLEASHING THOUGHT

Since writing is putting ideas down in written form, the first task is to help students to formulate ideas (or to think). For centuries philosophers have questioned what thinking really is, so how can we teach something that doesn't have a real definition? The answer is that we can't. We can guide, present models, suggest approaches. But the process of thinking is an internal, personal one that can be learned but not taught. How can we help students learn to think?

The POWER Process can help. Prewriting activities can unleash thought. Through discussion, students see that they do have ideas. Problem-solving activities allow them to think about ideas, beliefs, and feelings before they ever have to commit a word in writing. Prewriting leads to jotting down these ideas as notes for use later. Students can also keep journals or idea files on the word processor for future reference.

ADVANTAGES OF THE GROUP

Since the creative process is so elusive, students need time to think about their ideas in order to organize facts and experience around a particular topic for writing. Part of this preparatory stage involves testing their ideas against the thinking of others. Ideas are explored, enhanced, and focused in small-group settings because the fear of saying something foolish or incorrect is less when only a few people can hear. The groups should remain constant so students learn to trust the others.

Within the group, each member is both an editor and a writer. As an editor, a student discusses the work of others and makes suggestions. As a writer, he or she takes notes on the others' suggestions before making final plans for his or her own piece of writing. Eventually, it is time to write the first draft. Since word processing allows students to change what they have written easily, the blank screen is not the threat that the blank paper used to be. The writing step forces students to explain themselves, to organize their ideas and notes, and to express (and change) them as they think about what they are saying.

After the initial writing effort, students test their written ideas within their groups to see if others understand the logic of what they have said. Each person prints out enough copies for the group, and in the exchange stage, they question each others' beliefs, proof, and manner of expression. They also suggest improvements. The improvements can be made in the revision stage because a word processor makes the corrections easy to accomplish. Writers keep what was good and change what didn't work; they never recopy. The words on the screen aren't permanent the way indelible ink is. Only the final copy is turned in, and the group takes responsibility for helping each member to perfect his work. With a word processor, students can make several revisions and have the freedom to experiment with their words and ideas. The result is better copy.

NO MORE MESSY PAPERS

Another benefit of word processing is that it alleviates the frustration caused by poor handwriting. Students have been trained that the page must be neat and clean to be turned in. I have seen them copy over their work (not revise, simply copy) so that the appearance of the page is pretty. If their handwriting is poor, they concentrate on writing the symbols; thoughts are of lesser importance. If they mess up, they crumple the sheet and start over. Their feelings about their writing are inextricably tied to the appearance of the paper. If it doesn't look good, it isn't good. How many budding Hemingways are thwarted, ashamed of their work? Messy papers mean messy ideas.

With word processing, the appearance is always neat. Since students know that the paper will automatically be pretty, they are free to concentrate on what they want to say. The writing session won't end before they've had a chance to copy over. If the bell rings, they'll save what they've done and go back to fix it another day. Therefore, they understand that the finished product will be better. If they believe it will be better, and no longer have to penalize themselves for sloppiness, their work will indeed improve.

Perhaps we should not teach penmanship until students' motor coordination is good enough to handle it. What is the point of our present emphasis on penmanship in the lower grades? Adults seldom communicate anything of importance in handwritten words. And no matter how strange a scrawl may look to us, people can always read their own writing. Remembering the location of letters on a keyboard takes far less time to learn than producing letters of equal quality by hand.

WRITING FOR AN AUDIENCE

A word about publishing. Students traditionally write for the teacher. No one else reads what they have written, and the clever child knows what his teacher wants. His real perceptions and feelings are of little consequence, for writing is not really a means of expression. Rather, it is an attempt to put down on paper what the teacher wants to read.

When people write with the knowledge that others will read their work, there is a shift in the kind of effort they make. With word processing, it is a simple matter to create individual and class mini-magazines or to hang students' work on bulletin boards. In my experience, students can't wait to show off their finished work. Because it is legible, others can read it. Because others can read it, it will be read. If others read it, it is worth being read. That is the cycle of a student's feeling about his or her own written work. Students know that their classmates, friends, parents, and teachers will read their work. Their egos are enhanced by this knowledge. The experience of sharing what they have written provides positive reinforcement for the next piece of written work.

I like to call this sharing process the "bi-psych-le" theory of writing. Students have either good or bad feelings about themselves as human beings and as writers. Their feelings will be reinforced by external events because their perceptions of those events will be interpreted by their underlying feelings about themselves. It follows that when students feel good about their writing, they feel good about themselves. And every piece of writing they do, if they feel good about the process, will enhance their egos and reinforce their positive feelings about their writing. This is a cycle that can turn paper crumplers into positive thinkers.

ADVANTAGES FOR TEACHERS

The POWER Process has several effects on teachers, too. For one, as we see improvement in student writing, we begin to expect better work the next time. Students become aware of this and indeed begin to produce better work. So we get to read better papers. Traditionally, teachers are burdened with tests, compositions, book reports, and other examples of written work. Some work is illegible, most papers are not insightful, and almost all become boring after a while. With the POWER Process, we read only the final copy, a legible, revised document.

Another result of the POWER Process is that we become project managers and consultants. We lead the initial brainstorming and then consult with individuals and groups to provide assistance. The center of responsibility shifts from the teacher, teaching how to think and write, to the student (assisted by his group), internalizing the process of thinking and writing.

WRITING IN ALL DISCIPLINES

To reinforce the importance of writing, there should be what has been labeled "writing across the curriculum." What this means is that students should be encouraged to write in every subject area in order to improve their thinking skills in each area and to reinforce their writing skills. Sociological perspectives on history, the implications of a scientific experiment for the future, or the method of performing a mathematical task can all be expressed in writing. Since writing is thinking, students who write in all subjects will internalize thinking skills in all subjects.

The process of writing involves applying technical verbal skills to the process of thinking. The writer considers how to handle ideas, what the ideas mean, what is the most logical order for these ideas, and a host of other problems. Solving these problems means thinking. When a student asks of another, "Why won't this argument convince you that my idea is right?" both are learning logic and persuasion. The interchange of ideas and the refinement of thinking that follows are what promote learning.

Chapter 5
Are Computers a Panacea?

Most of us will admit that there are problems with the educational system today. Several reports released recently have found education in America to be wanting. What does it want? Well, it seems that students are notably lacking in logical thinking skills and in the ability to communicate effectively. These are high-priority items on the agenda for educational reform. What do computers have to do with school reform? Well, computers are the biggest thing to hit our society since the discovery that peanut butter and jelly sandwiches don't only taste good but are nutritious too. More and more computers are in the schools and more and more teachers are being trained to use them. The question is this: How should we use these computers as educational tools?

There are four computer-related topics to which students can be introduced: the cultural significance of computers; programming; computer-assisted instruction; and applications of computer technology such as word processing. When we think about which of these computer-related topics to emphasize in our classrooms, we really have to look at the end result: How will each of these uses of the computer affect learning?

THE SOCIAL AND ECONOMIC IMPORTANCE OF COMPUTERS

One of the most important areas for investigation is the relationship of computers to our world. Micros didn't spring up overnight, and students should be aware of their beginnings. If we call our age the technological revolution, it should be studied with the same vigor as the industrial revolution. Students should learn of the social, scientific, mathematical, and historical issues that surround computers and electronic technology.

COMPUTER PROGRAMMING

Programming is another area for learning. Students should be encouraged to understand how the computer does its job. By learning to program, students learn the importance of a logical progression of instructions. They can also exercise control over this phenomenon of modern technology and feel a sense of power with its mastery. However, the mania to train every student as a potential programmer is silly. Fewer programmers will be needed in the future than now; BASIC—the language most commonly taught today—is not a particularly professional language, and most people can benefit from computer use without knowing how to program the machine. The thrust of computer-literacy courses should really be to teach students how a computer can help us to learn and how we can use it to improve our lives.

COMPUTER-ASSISTED INSTRUCTION

Computer-assisted instruction (CAI) is used in many classrooms. In a nutshell, there are four different types of instruction-assistance programs. *Drill and Practice* is what the term implies, multiple exercises in a given skill area (such as addition or spelling). *Tutorials* combine drill with instruction, often reviewing a concept after only a few errors have been made. *Simulations* provide a situation (usually scientific or historical) in which students try to find the best course of action. *Discovery* software encourages conceptual thinking; students learn a process by using it.

There are good, bad, and indifferent programs in each of these categories, and there are many examples of each. For the most part, *simulations* and *discovery* software help students learn to think. The other types reinforce specific skills. These programs are all widely used, yet we still don't have evidence that computer-assisted instruction is the best use of computers. Before we decide how helpful this kind of computer use is, let's look a little more closely at the different kinds of CAI software.

Drill and Practice

There is a vast market of *drill-and-practice* programs; some are quite good, and others are electronic page turners. There is a certain value to all of them because of the interactive nature of the machine itself and the fact that it is an infinitely patient teacher. A question is posed; the student can deliberate until he is ready to answer. The computer will never call on another student in the interim or urge speed. There is positive reinforcement as well. Most programs will reward a correct answer with a congratulatory message (some even provide graphics or sound as reinforcement), and then the student proceeds to the next question. If the student's response was incorrect, no one criticizes; he is urged to try again.

Tutorials

Tutorials provide instruction to guide the student in his selection of answers. This infinitely patient teacher will even reinforce the same concept with numerous examples, or pick up the lesson on another day if the student cannot handle more right now. Sometimes instruction is given first; sometimes it reappears when the student answers several questions incorrectly. Review is often provided as well.

The Language Arts topics that are available in both drill-and-practice and tutorial software include alphabet skills (both for young children and for older students' alphabetizing practice); mechanical skills such as capitalization and punctuation; and grammatical concepts such as parts of speech, sentence combining, sentence structure, and agreement. Training or practice in other technical skills is available on disk as well. Vocabulary and spelling programs abound; some even let the teacher enter his or her own words. Just remember, though, this is drill in isolation. The student going through a vocabulary exercise on a computer is not necessarily integrating the words into his or her own personal vocabulary. Your students can have fun doing crossword puzzles and unscrambling words, however, if that is your goal. There are also some highly structured programs that will drill students on material for the SAT exam. Since the exam itself is in a multiple-choice format, a college-bound student can gain considerable benefit from this software, learning to be comfortable with the type of question and the level of difficulty characteristic of the SAT. Some of these programs also provide explanations of the topics covered or errors made.

Simulations

A third type of CAI provides a different experience. One of the best ways to internalize information is to use it, and while it is difficult to use scientific or historical facts in daily life, *simulation* software can give students an opportunity to do just that. *Simulations* teach the problem-solving approach to a particular concept or event. A situation is presented and students must decide on a course of action, which in turn leads them to further analysis, decision-making, and learning from the results of their decisions. While this variety of software is more common in science and social studies classrooms, there are also simulations available for the Language Arts teacher. Some of these involve exercises in logical thinking, strategy development and pattern-recognition. With these programs students learn by doing, which is the essence of learning. My mother used to say, "Oh, go ahead. You'll learn from your own mistakes." She was right; I never learned what people told me was the right thing to do; I learned by doing (and doing wrong very often). I saw firsthand what worked and what didn't; then I was wiser the next time. Children haven't changed since I was young; to experiment and to extrapolate from that trial-and-error process is human nature. So simulations provide a valuable opportunity to test decision-making and problem-solving skills and to learn from the attempt.

Discovery Software

Discovery software also gives children an opportunity to learn by doing. The best known example of *discovery* software is *Rocky's Boots* (published by The Learning Company). Students build machines (through trial and error) that conduct electricity. They can then use their machines in various ways. LOGO—a programming language—is another example of the teaching-through-discovery possibilities of the computer. Using LOGO, the child learns patterns, shapes, geometry, and logical progression by moving a turtle around the screen. The philosophy behind LOGO (developed by Seymour Papert at MIT) is the Piagetian idea that children learn by discovering, by doing.

More programs of this variety are being released. And many of them could be considered discovery-based or guided-discovery software. I believe these are the most valuable kinds of CAI software. If the student is using his skills to learn and is learning by experimenting, the computer time that makes this achievement possible is truly time well spent.

COMPUTER-ASSISTED INSTRUCTION: AN ASSESSMENT

The same cannot necessarily be said for *all* kinds of computer-assisted instruction, however. Considering that there is a limit to the amount of time we have available for computer use in the classroom, we need to be very careful in our decisions about the programs our students will use. *Drill-and-practice* and *tutorial* programs, for instance, are of such specific, limited value that they should almost never be used for a whole class at once. Why should a student practice comma use if he or she already uses commas correctly—or still hasn't mastered periods and question marks? On the other hand, if a student's writing repeatedly shows misunderstanding of the grammatical principle that pronouns should agree in number and person with their antecedents, a CAI package addressed to this concept may be just what is needed. The most appropriate use of CAI, in other words, is as individualized reinforcement according to student need. As long as our access to computers is limited, we must take care that we use these machines for kinds of teaching that *can't* be just as well accomplished with blackboards and workbooks—that we use our computers to teach skills and concepts a computer is uniquely suited to teach.

COMPUTER APPLICATIONS

The fourth area of computer use includes such practical *applications* as word processors, spreadsheets, and file managers. While these are used in business, they can also serve students well. In the process of using applications software, students don't only improve learning but also become familiar with programs that are commonly used in the real world.

A tool such as word processing can help students to think logically, write creatively, and communicate effectively. File-management programs can be used in conjunction with word processing for reports, notes, and other information for the writer. And spreadsheets can be used to learn projections and forecasting. It is in the use of these practical applications that students will gain the most from classroom computers.

Word processing, because it frees students from the mechanical drudgery of writing, is an excellent means to teach writing skills. Because students can insert, delete, and move text, they are free to create, to think logically, to communicate, and to impose form and mechanics at whatever point in their thinking/writing process they are comfortable. In addition, there are word processing accessories that will help students to accomplish related tasks.

Through prewriting and group analysis exercises, students learn skills that they can then apply in lots of other academic areas. As they help another student focus on his or her main idea, for example, they learn to check their own work for its main idea. Later the skill of identifying a main idea will carry over into their reading of other texts as well. What we are talking about is no longer reading taught as a subject unto itself; it is reading for personal use.

Software also exists that attempts to teach writing skills. While using a word processor to go through the actual process of writing is the best way to learn, some of these programs can supply ideas and techniques to supplement instruction. There are story starters, idea generators, logic trees, and diary programs to help. Since these allow for student expression (and are really enhanced word processors), they are more versatile than traditional CAI material. Some encourage student manipulation of language, some prompt for ideas or form. There is even an entire outlining, writing, revising package that is being used in some schools. There are other ways to improve student knowledge and skills that can also be considered computer applications. With the addition of a modem, students can link up with information services, with bulletin boards, and with other people. All subject areas can be affected by this use.

In reality, our goal with computers in education is to help students to learn by using methods that are superior to those that have been used in the past. Not every possible computer application is appropriate in the classroom. If computers are going to be a real force in education, they must be used wisely. Obviously, from the focus of this book, I believe that the best use of computers in the classroom is in the Language Arts curriculum to teach students how to write well.

Chapter 6
The Language Arts Curriculum

Just what is Language Arts, or English, anyway? Called by both titles, the subject is intangible. Why would anyone in his right mind want to teach an intangible to children? Well, literature is "the stuff that dreams are made of"; its subject matter is the world, and the methodology of English teaching involves having students think. English is the most fascinating of subjects to teach, really.

WHY TEACH ENGLISH?

The Language Arts curriculum is the world of the past, the present, and the future. Students read great literature not only to develop an appreciation of others' words, but also to experience catharsis and to relate what they have read to their own lives and to the world around them. From literature students also learn the most important skill for living, that of communicating well. In English, they learn how to express themselves properly in writing and in speaking. After all, giving directions in the right order and specifying details are necessary skills. I think we can be fair saying that the purpose of English is to provide skills for living well.

The English curriculum involves a complex array of specialized skills which all people need, including reading, writing, speech, grammar, spelling, and vocabulary. The experience known as English or Language Arts integrates these subtopics in order to help students learn to think and to communicate.

WHY TEACH WRITING?

Since the topic of this book is the teaching of writing through word processing, I will explain how all of the subtopics above are related to the process of writing. First of all, writing involves several proficiencies: in grammar and usage, in spelling, and in vocabulary, most notably. Speaking well is the ability to communicate ideas. If students learn how to present ideas in writing, they will be able to present ideas logically for oral delivery as well. Reading abilities, too, can be enhanced through instruction in writing as we use literature to promote thinking and to find models for writing. What we really try to teach when we teach writing are the abilities to think logically and to express these thoughts and ideas.

TEACHING GRAMMAR

Grammar as traditionally taught is an exercise in futility. There is little point in making students memorize the names of parts of speech or parts of a sentence, because there is little if any carry-over into student writing when grammar is learned in isolation. After all, improvement in student speech and writing is the only point of teaching correct usage. Grammatical concepts should be taught as needed. Students in a given class tend to make the same types of errors, and when it is evident that several students are weak in a particular area, we can address that relevant concept in a lesson.

As far as students are concerned, grammar is irrelevant, immaterial and ignoble. Is there anything else that will cause so many groans? To make sense, grammar and usage must be put into perspective. What do I do with this? What is the point of learning it?

Grammar is not an end in itself, as you would believe from perusing any grammar text or workbook. Exercises requiring students to fill in the blanks are wasted effort. The only way students will relate grammar and usage to their own writing is if the teacher shows them how. Teach grammar by using models that demonstrate the concept. Let students devise their own examples of correct use of the concept. Then, whether the principle being taught concerns sentence structure or punctuation, they will internalize its use.

In any lesson on grammar, the final step should be for students to examine their own writing for applications of the concept presented. They should ask themselves, how could my work be improved based on the element of grammar or usage I have learned? Only when students apply the concepts to their own writing will they learn grammar and usage for more than a few moments.

TEACHING LITERATURE

Works of literature should be used as models. Obviously, for every writing topic in the modules here examples can be found in literature, and anthologies provide examples of most. When literature and writing are taught in conjunction with each other, students acquire a better understanding of both. Literature becomes material to analyze, a model of ideas and techniques for one's own work. It is no longer "the classics," dusty works to revere and fear. As students learn to read literature and to read their own work in the context of a particular style or technique, literature will become part of their own base of information.

TEACHING THROUGH OTHER MEDIA

Media can be used in the teaching of writing as well. Radio, TV, newspapers, and magazines are models, and you and your students can provide samples. Students can tape record radio broadcasts, capture television programs on a VCR, and bring in newspapers and magazines. Each form of writing can be used as a model against which students can compare their own efforts.

TEACHING SPELLING AND VOCABULARY

Spelling and vocabulary, whether derived from literature or from lists, should be integrated into the students' work. When a word is used in speech or in writing, it becomes part of the user's vocabulary. Students can keep lists of words they encounter and will use in their writing; they can invent sentence and paragraph games on the word processor; or they can use words as story or idea starters. The key to vocabulary development is use. The more often a word is used, the more likely it is to become part of a student's own, personal vocabulary.

TEACHING ORAL COMMUNICATION

Oral communication can be correlated with its written counterpart. As students work in groups to improve their writing, thinking skills improve. This improvement will be as evident in student speech as in their writing. As they perfect expository writing, for example, they can select topics for debate as prewriting activities or present completed essays to engender discussion.

TEACHING READING

Although the ability to read and to use comprehension skills is treated as a separate entity in many school districts, it is really part of the Language Arts curriculum. Reading improvement will occur with writing improvement. As students read each other's work, reading skills improve. They learn what to look for in writing and how to follow the logic in any given text. As soon as they internalize the procedure for analyzing the work of other group members, they will approach any written material with the same skills.

Chapter 7
Writing Across the Curriculum

When I chose the title for this chapter, I had a vision of stacks of curriculum guides with scribbling all over the covers. Maybe that image is a symbol of what I'd like to change in subjects other than English. I'll explain: Mathematics and science are measurable subjects; to some extent history is as well. For each of these, there is a body of facts that can be taught and tested. That's a neat package and I guess I'm jealous. English can't be tested objectively.

But that's precisely the strength of English—that it involves comprehension of the whole world around us. Since perception of that world is open to interpretation, we can't mark students' opinions right or wrong (as long as they back up what they say). Perhaps the other academic subjects should be taught in the same way. Students must learn the facts and concepts, but only if they *use* the facts and concepts in their writing, will they learn a perspective on that information as well. By analyzing subject matter in the writing process, students can make it part of their working base of knowledge.

WRITING OPPORTUNITIES OUTSIDE THE ENGLISH CLASS

To be sure, English teachers use social and historical issues for writing topics, but everything can be a topic for writing, and the people most on top of "everything" are subject-area teachers. Actually there has been a push to have students write in every class. I guess it began a few years ago with signs and posters declaring, "Every class is an English class." But announcements don't help; to be effective, a teacher has to know how to use a particular technique or philosophy. If subject-area teachers themselves haven't been trained to write, they won't be comfortable writing or requiring their students to do it. The result of the "English class" program was that subject-area teachers reluctantly added an essay question to the end of their short-answer tests.

We can encourage subject-area teachers to write and to assign written work. We can also suggest ways in which writing can be used to further subject-area learning and hope that subject teachers will develop and enlarge these suggestions. But unless we conduct massive workshops to train all teachers in the process of writing, we can only pray for the best.

We don't want every class to be an English class; each class should simply create a learning situation where students consider the subject matter of a particular discipline and express their understanding in writing. This practice can promote an educational system where facts are not isolated bits of information, but rather are integrated into students' usable knowledge. After all, that is our purpose: that students should internalize academic subject matter so that they gain true understanding that merges with everything else they think, see, and know.

What I offer below is a series of suggestions about specific kinds of writing that can be used easily in any subject. If subject teachers can use word processing and the POWER Process with their classes, they may want to create mini-magazines, theme journals, newspapers, and bulletin boards. When they and their students enjoy writing, the processes of writing and learning become one.

VOCABULARY

Each subject has its own vocabulary, and every subject teacher is familiar with assigning technical or specialized words for students to learn. However, subject-area vocabulary is no more a part of the students' normal word list than isolated words they encounter for a single purpose anywhere. Memorizing vocabulary does not make the words the students' own.

It is helpful for students to write each word, its definition, and a sentence illustrating its meaning, but they'll still forget the words when the test or the term is over. Instead of studying each word in isolation from the others, could they perhaps write passages which use the specialized vocabulary to explain a concept? Could they relate the concept to the whole subject area? Can they write creatively about math, science, and social studies?

For example, I might write an essay pretending I am a blood vessel in my body. What's my name? My job? Who are my co-workers and neighbors? How do I eat, sleep, and breathe? And what is my relationship to that gurgling stomach and pounding heart that keep me awake at night? Am I in a sheltered environment or is the air outside part of my existence too? Above all, what words have special meaning to me? (Please don't take this in vein.)

SUMMARIES

Students are used to summarizing information in small enough segments so they can handle and understand concepts. Summaries also can include notes or lists of facts or details to be used for dramatizations of historical events. ("Yes, Mr. Jackson, the kitchen cabinet has arrived; just wait 'till you see what's cooking.")

Scientific discoveries and dates to remember can be "current events" written as leads for a period newspaper. ("Extra, extra, read all about it; steam engine isn't all hot air.") Not one to shortchange mathematics, I need a summary of the steps to draw a hopscotch field for my sidewalk geometry club. Summaries of battles and inventions can be great for how-to articles. Students can even write talk-show scripts using summaries of scientific or historical events.

ANALYSIS

There are always several ways to analyze any issue or topic. One student may see an invention, for example, as several pieces of equipment becoming a whole, while another will see the historical necessity behind that invention. A third will focus on the scientific method that made the discovery possible. Students analyze particular concepts from their own perspectives and can explain their ways of looking at the concept in writing.

Why must we know how to find the area of a circle or a rectangle? Or how big are the pizza and chocolate bar? If I belonged to a family of ants, how many of us could fit on that Boston cream pie?

EXPLANATIONS

Everyone writes directions and gives explanations; the step-by-step method of doing something is valuable in every subject area. In mathematics, how to solve a problem or do an equation can be expressed in writing; in fact, the writing process helps foster a real understanding of the concept or technique. In science, a description of how to conduct a particular experiment or an explanation of how electricity or photosynthesis works can further understanding. In hygiene, students can demonstrate in writing how to revive someone with CPR or how to bandage a wound. In history, students can explain how to start a war or win or lose one. In art, students can describe how to draw perspective or prepare papier-mâché. In music, they can consider how to play a tune or understand Bach. In foreign language, they can write any sort of essay in that language, or they can tell how to see the sights in a city where the foreign language is spoken.

DESCRIPTIONS

Everything that exists can be described. Students can describe any object in several different ways depending on the subject area. (A leaf is different to a scientist than it is to an artist.) Students can describe a paramecium, a platypus, a pterodactyl, the battlefield at Ypres, a wounded patient (and how to help him, please), a palette, or a piano. I hate to belabor the point, but for a piece of creative writing a student could even *be* a soldier on the battlefield, a sparkling streak of crimson acrylic (how did he ever turn that hue?), or a bee doing what comes naturally. Everything appeals to one sense or another (sometimes only nonsense), and if he or she explains it in writing, the student will be helped to learn.

BIOGRAPHY

Every subject area has figures of importance. Mathematicians, scientists, historical personages of every variety can all be used for biographical sketches. Why did George Washington have wooden teeth? Why did William Howard Taft need a new bathtub? Sometimes learning about the absurd in history makes the past more real. There are people who lived, breathed, slept, ate, and did all of the same boring things we do, but we've never seen them as real people. The first woman pirate, for example. Or the man who fired the shot heard round the world. Did Abe's mother really like the log cabin? ("You can't move, Mother; it's part of my image to the voters.") Or what did George really say after the cherry tree fell? (##$%%$%!!!)

EVALUATIONS

Students often don't see the value of particular scientific, mathematical, or historical concepts in relation to their lives. If they are asked to relate events in writing or to write about the relevance of a concept, they will see where the curriculum and life fit together. Let's add some gravity to this chapter. If Isaac Newton never lived, would I be standing on my head? How did those guys in space defy Isaac's laws? And what did Isaac's mother say when he came home with a bump on his head?

PERSUASION

Every mathematical and scientific discovery, every historical situation had detractors at the time. Students can ride a time warp to be citizens of a different age. They can take sides at the Scopes trial, be a juror or a columnist. Why should we build a transcontinental railroad? Can Orville come down from the clouds? Should we dig for gold in them thar hills? Yes or no? Take a stand, students, and convince us that history was right or wrong.

FICTION

Students can invent dialogue and use the history available to write "fictionalized" versions of events. Remember "You Are There" on television? They can change one fact and speculate about how the world would be different. ("I guess you're right, Lewis, Oregon can't be this way.") What if Copernicus had had dirt on his telescope? Or Betsy Ross had liked a different pattern?

QUESTIONS

In order to understand some topics, students can be asked to make up "essay" questions they think should be asked on a test. For review, they can answer each other's questions and discuss the results. You can even give them their own questions on a test and chuckle all the way home with the papers.

RESEARCH

Of course, the research paper is already a part of many classes. And while we generally want students to address a serious issue in their research papers, we can occasionally direct them to some exotic truths to explore. How did Dolly Madison make history (herstory)? Who was the power behind the throne? What is Machiavelli's influence today? Whether serious or irreverent, the narratives that students write become meaningful to them. Suddenly, subjects they questioned having to take are relevant to their lives. You know what else? They're learning.

Chapter 8

Word Processing Software and Accessories

Software is like any other tool—the right one helps you get the job done the best. Yet there are several hundred word-processing programs on the market; so how should you decide which is best for you and for your students? Some word-processing programs are easy to learn and easy to use; most of these have basic text-editing features and few frills. Then there are programs that take more effort; these usually have features you won't need right away but may welcome as your own sophistication grows. In general, the easier the program is to learn and use, the fewer advanced features are possible with it. The reason for this has to do with computer memory, but exactly how that works isn't important here.

TWO KINDS OF SOFTWARE

Two varieties of word processing software exist: menu- and command-driven. In English, that means you either have options listed somewhere on the screen and you can press a key to choose among them, or you have to know what combination of special keys will get your computer to do its tricks. Let's look at an example. With a menu-driven program, when you want to save your document, you locate the SAVE option on the screen and press RETURN. With a command-driven program, you hold down the CONTROL key and press a letter key that tells your computer, "Get ready to save my text." Clever programs use mnemonic cues such as CONTROL-S for save. A menu-driven program will ask you to give your document a filename; a command-driven program will put a symbol on the screen that you have to know means to give your document a filename. For example, "Save:" might appear in a corner. With both types of word processors, you must type a filename and press RETURN.

An important feature of word processors in general is that they should be as invisible as possible. You should be able to create without thinking about the word processor. Initially, menu-driven programs are superior; the novice types to his heart's content and then selects options from the screen to change his text. After a little use, command-driven programs are superior; the commands become automatic (sometimes they're even listed at the top of the screen), and you don't need to take the time to read familiar instructions.

For young children, menu-driven programs are probably the best. There's nothing for them to remember or think about except the words and ideas they create. For older children (and adults), command-driven programs are better; commands for simple features are learned easily, and more complex features can be learned or taught as needed. Let's look at some examples of word processors that cost under $100.

Menu-Driven Software

Bank Street Writer, available from both Scholastic and Broderbund, is the original children's menu-driven word processor. It is available for Apple, Atari, Commodore 64, and IBM computers. *Bank Street* is easy to learn and easy to use; on-screen prompts provide almost all the help needed, but there are few sophisticated features for advanced students. Children enter and delete text in the WRITE mode, but only in EDIT mode can they move the cursor around the screen. Also in the EDIT mode, children can select from several other options: ERASE, UNERASE, MOVE, MOVEBACK, FIND, and REPLACE. They can also enter the TRANSFER mode, which allows them to SAVE, RETRIEVE, REMOVE, or RENAME a text file, or to PRINT a draft or final copy of their work.

The Milliken Word Processor, a newer menu-driven program for Apple computers, competes with *Bank Street*. Basic word-processing features such as entering text, moving the cursor, and inserting and deleting, are all performed in a single mode. Other options become available when the writer presses ESC to display the main menu, and then selects the desired submenu. Single keystrokes accomplish most functions, and large letters and prompts above the text area make this system easy for very young children to use. Like *Bank Street, Milliken* offers few sophisticated word-processing features. Unfortunately, once you DELETE a block, you can't change your mind, and the FIND command (there's no RE-PLACE) is awkward to use. This program is part of a series that includes on-screen assistance in the writing process, a spelling checker, and other welcome features on additional disks at additional cost.

HomeWord, from Sierra On-Line, is a menu-driven program with pictures that runs on Apple, Atari, Commodore 64, and IBM computers. You enter text, move the cursor, insert, and delete in a single mode. Other functions are selected through menus and submenus, all available through icons (pictures). As children learn the options available to them—and there are some fairly sophisticated word-processing features—they can use direct commands. Advanced capabilities include replacing text by striking over; underlining; adding bold-face type, headings, and footers; and aligning text. You can also move or copy whole blocks of text, search for a word and replace it with another, and link two or more documents together.

Cut & Paste, by Electronic Arts, also runs on Apple, Atari, Commodore 64, and IBM computers. As a basic, inexpensive, menu-driven word processor, it is versatile and easy for children to learn and to use. Prompts and user-friendly messages help you do what you want and alert you when you might do something that could be a mistake. Direct commands are possible when students become familiar with the program. Sophisticated features include strikeovers, controlling page breaks, and printing paragraphs without leaving the first or last line on a page by itself. (Lines so left are sometimes called widows and orphans.) Unfortunately, this system does not offer the options to search for and to replace a word.

The document disk for *Cut & Paste* contains samples of commonly used forms: letters, outline, memo, resume, and envelope. These can be used as models for student work, or children can superimpose their own text over the samples.

Command-Driven Software

A command-driven program like *The Write Choice*, by Roger Wagner Publishing for Apple computers, is more difficult to learn than menu-driven software. Many of the commands in this word processor are not obvious. For example, though it is fairly obvious that CONTROL-B stands for "beginning," it is not so easy to remember that CONTROL-R stands for "delete," even when you think "remove."

The Write Choice has several advantages, though. Screen display is the same as what will appear on the printed page. Centering, underlining, and special formatting are possible. Other, more sophisticated features, such as chaining documents and recovering files, are also available as the level of student sophistication grows. In addition, students who need practice with touch typing can use the *Write Choice's* typing tutor or the game on the reverse side of that disk. Those who need reminders of business-letter form and correct usage will appreciate the assistance of print materials provided in this package as well.

The Writer, from Hayden, also for Apple computers, is an inexpensive, command-driven word processor that is difficult to learn. Yet it is versatile, and if teachers are willing to invest the time to learn it themselves, they can teach it to older students. Prompts and a control-code summary are listed on the top portion of the screen; this help is essential, because control keys are not mnemonic cues and cannot be remembered easily. To determine margins and other formatting choices for your printed page, you put the print commands within the text. And you can display on the screen how the pages will look when printed out. There are some sophisticated features available, such as word count and appending files, but they are not easy to use.

Designed and written by teachers and researchers, *The Writer's Assistant*, from InterLearn, is an extremely valuable and versatile program for Apple computers. It has the power of command-driven software and the ease of use of menu-driven word processors. Young children can work at the novice level and adults can make use of the advanced features at the expert level.

Writing and editing are completed in a single mode with the help of single-keystroke commands; no control key is needed. Prompts at the top of the screen indicate the many options. Screen margins can be set to the same width as print format. Other features include inserting, deleting, and copying text, striking over, aligning or rearranging text, and global search and replace. Unlike other word processors for children, *The Writer's Assistant* includes a spelling checker for the 100 most commonly misspelled words. The printed page can be designed with commands placed within the text or from a menu of options. There are numerous features, including headers, footers, underlining, subscripts and superscripts, overstrike, and appending files. This is a stand-alone word processor, but compatible software for reading and writing development and for communicating with other computers over telephone lines is available separately. The *Writer's Assistant* is the text editor used in the *Quill* writing program, another package that includes help with the process of writing.

Many schools have TRS-80 computers, so it's really a shame that there is no easy-to-use word processor for these machines. I used *Scripsit*, a Radio Shack product, with my students. Other people prefer *Electric Pencil*, from IJG (It's Just Great), for the classroom. Actually, there isn't all that much difference between them. Both are command-driven, and neither offers on-screen help. *Electric Pencil* comes with a tear-out reference card to help you remember commands; *Scripsit* comes with labels to stick onto the front of your keys. The biggest difference is that *Scripsit* is more difficult to learn because you have to sit through hours of an audio cassette tutorial. Once you've done that, the rest is easy, and the system is easy enough to teach to a class. *Electric Pencil's* manual is a self-guided tutorial, but you'll still have to instruct students about how to use the program. With both programs, you replace letters as you type over old ones, and you can move the cursor around the screen. To do anything else (like insert or delete), you need commands. Both are perfectly adequate programs. *Pencil* may be a little easier to operate, but *Scripsit* has more advanced features. The biggest difference is in cost; *Scripsit* is twice as expensive as *Electric Pencil*.

When I bought my Apple IIe computer, *AppleWriter II*, which was designed for the Apple II and II Plus machines, was a bonus (?) from my dealer. So I used it. I complained a lot because it didn't do things as easily as I was used to with *Scripsit* on the TRS-80. When I got annoyed enough to spend money to solve my problems, I bought *AppleWriter IIe*, which is expensive. I chose it because it's extremely versatile and it could also read the text files I had already written. I've gotten used to it and rarely think about the few things it can't do. It has commands that are easy to remember, help screens, and many text-editing and print-formatting features. It also comes with a word-processing language that I can understand and that allows me to do interesting things.

INSTRUCTION MANUALS

A word about manuals: many of them are complicated to understand. In general, the menu-driven word processors have instruction guides that are easier to follow. When you're a novice, it seems as if the manuals that accompany most command-driven word processors go overboard on explaining things, but when you get used to the program, you find it helps to understand what you're doing and how.

Selecting a word processor is a difficult task; all of them give you the same basic features, but they vary in how easy they are to learn and use. Some offer sophisticated features that you may want later. For fun, try looking at ten different programs (as I just did to write this chapter) and see if you can remember anything about any of them when you've finished.

WORD-PROCESSING ACCESSORIES

Throughout this book I've applauded word processing as the ultimate tool for teaching writing, yet I'm about to discuss accessories. What more could we need? To begin with, for report writing, we need a way to record and store notes. File cards will do, and so will a word processor set up with files for each topic. However, I'd like to mention other software we can use to get this job done faster and better. Whatever accessories you use, you must be sure that they can work together with your word processor. Most accessories will specify which programs they're compatible with, but file managers and spreadsheets have a life of their own, so you have to ask before you buy. There are some combination programs like *AppleWorks* that include a word processor, a file manager, and a spreadsheet all in one package.

File Managers

File-management programs are very popular in business, and students can use them for reports in any subject since they are really file cabinets on disk. Each time students want to add information on a topic, they load that file into the computer and enter their notes. When the notes are complete, students can sort them in any order they need. Then they use the word processor to assemble the facts and write the report.

Spreadsheets

Students can use spreadsheet programs to keep business records for companies they create in mathematics. They can record the costs of raw materials, the profit desired, and the expenses, and then can update any or all of the items. Students can see projections for future sales and do inventory control. Then they can use their facts and figures to correspond with clients and suppliers and to create annual reports on the word processor.

Spelling Checkers

We are talking about writing, however, and aside from the classroom applications of business software, there are programs that work with word processors to improve the mechanics of writing. Not one of these is essential, but they can help students to catch unnoticed errors. The most popular variety of word-processing accessory is the dictionary, or spelling checker. This kind of program will pick up misspellings and typos. The student's text is compared to a list of words in the program, and the errors appear on the screen. Some programs will run through the text and provide a list of misspelled (or mistyped) words at the end. Students must then go through their work to find the errors and correct them. More sophisticated dictionary programs highlight errors in context and allow for immediate changes. Some programs will even suggest alternate spellings for words (either phonetically or alphabetically).

Spelling checkers, used when students revise, can help them recognize their spelling errors. They can look up the offending words and learn the proper spelling for the future. There is only one problem. Students may use technical or colloquial words, which will show up as errors because they are not listed in the program. Some software takes this problem into account and allows you to add your own words to the list.

Style Checkers

Another popular type of accessory is the grammar or style checker. The student's text is compared to a set of rules and the errors appear on the screen. Students can double-check their punctuation and grammar while they revise. Some of these style checkers spot awkward expressions, incorrect usage, clichés, and wordiness. Students mark the errors on a printout and go back into the text to edit. Some of the style-check programs indicate the type of error that was made; this feature can help students locate the areas in which they need practice.

Thesaurus Programs

There are also thesaurus programs available. These can help students find synonyms and avoid overusing a particular word. Students still must know the connotation of the synonym, or they may choose an inappropriate word. Other than saving students the effort of looking up the word themselves, a computerized thesaurus offers no real advantage (other than speed) over a paperback Roget.

Word Counters

There are also programs that are perhaps more useful to professional writers. Some software will make word counts (determining either the frequency of use of a particular word or the total word count). There are programs that will index and cross-reference text, and some software will create a table of contents, footnotes, and bibliographies. Another type of software is the idea or outline planner, which gives prompts to help the writer focus on his topic and subtopics in a logical, orderly way.

Some of these accessories can be of real assistance in the classroom; others are probably not worth the expense. However, new items appear daily, and it is possible that some of the features being developed will deserve use in the classroom. In fact, it is likely that an encyclopedia will be available on disk within the next year. Pre-writing activities in the subject areas will then be able to include encyclopedia research for topic selection.

One last area to consider is technically not software, but it has tremendous potential in the classroom. This technological development is called telecommunications, and it uses computers and telephone lines for transmitting and retrieving information. To accomplish telecommunications, you need a computer, an open telephone line, a modem (device to change computer signals to telephone signals), and software (usually packaged with the modem) that allows you to contact other computers from yours.

With this equipment, students can use information retrieval services to do library and other research, send school newspapers to other schools, and exchange information and ideas (in writing, of course) with students in far-off places. The future use of computers through the power of telecommunications has many possibilities for educational purposes.

Chapter 9
Out of the Mouths of Experts

Somehow, every book on education seems to get to the point of a "review of the literature." (The literature consists of books and articles others have written which prove the point the author wants to make.) For the most part, quotes are boring, so I've assembled all of mine in one chapter and saved it for last. If this kind of stuff annoys you, you can skip this part.

Before you start turning pages, though, I'd like to offer some comments on writing this chapter from the point of view of a cut-and-paste term-paper writer. Whenever I've gone to school (for a degree or even for a single course), the inevitable term paper has been assigned. Except in isolated instances, I haven't viewed these assignments as particularly creative. So my approach has always been to cut and paste. Generally I've read whatever material my research has turned up and taken notes on file cards. When I've had enough of that, I've found the largest work space available (usually the floor) and put the cards into order. (The cards for each segment of the paper have had their own piece of the floor.) Then, very carefully, I've paper clipped and rubber banded the piles.

Then the writing has begun. I've taken a pack of cards and carefully invented transition phrases, sentences, and paragraphs so the notes on one card would lead to the notes on the next. And so forth and so on. I've hardly ever wasted a card, either. I used to figure that if I'd read and taken notes on something, it was going to be a footnote. The footnote proved I had done the work. This system may have been horrendous intellectually, but it made me happy as a compulsive organizer. My professors never seemed to notice or object, either.

Writing this chapter gave me my first chance to cite references with a word processor. My original method is so ingrained that I still used the file-card routine, but the rest of the work was different. I dutifully entered my notes into various disk files and then tried to merge them with my usual transitions. But the whole process changed. I moved things around, said more on my own, and quoted less.

Then of course I edited out a lot of what I had written to make the chapter more readable. (My college professors wouldn't have to suffer as much if all their students used word processors.) In the process, I absorbed much more of what I had taken notes on than my old system would have allowed.

So three cheers for word processing term papers. If you're curious about how the method worked, you can continue reading this chapter.

I'll begin by telling why I wrote this book. For one thing, like many other English teachers, I had noticed a decline in my students' ability to write well. When two major studies on education in the United States made the same observation, I felt free to state my opinions aloud. The studies were my footnotes; if they said it, I must be right.

Another thing happened. I fell in love with computers and, because of them, evolved a method that I really believe can help students write better. Others were making similar discoveries so, again, I had sources to prove my point.

The National Commission on Excellence in Education drew attention to the problem by claiming that "many 17-year-olds do not possess the 'higher order' intellectual skills we should expect of them" and "only one-fifth can write a persuasive essay."[1] That's quite a condemnation. The Commission went on to say the solution to this problem requires teaching high school English so that students will be able to "(a) comprehend, interpret, evaluate, and use what they read and (b) write well-organized, effective papers."[2] These are great performance objectives; what's missing is method. The best method for teaching students to think and write is exactly what those of us out there in the classrooms have been trying to figure out.

We do get a pat on the back from Ernest Boyer of the Carnegie Commission; he recognizes that we are working to help students learn. He too sees a deficiency in student abilities, and links thinking and writing skills: "Thought and language are inextricably connected . . . as students become more proficient in self-expression, the quality of their thinking also will improve."[3] For the Carnegie Commission, "the first curriculum priority is language. It is the most essential tool for learning."[4]

Thus, from the Carnegie Commission we can learn how valuable English teachers are in the scheme of things, but the question of method remains unanswered. My instinct recently has been to look to computers for the answers, and if you read the other chapters in this book, you see how my thinking has progressed from computers in general to word processing and the writing process in particular. Fortunately, both Boyer and the National Commission also understand that computers should be used as tools. Boyer believes, "Learning with computers means helping students study specific subjects and improve their skills in areas such

---

[1] The National Commission on Excellence in Education, *A Nation At Risk: The Imperative for Educational Reform* (Washington D.C.: U.S. Government Printing Office, 1983), p. 9.

[2] *Ibid.*, p. 25.

[3] Ernest Boyer, *High School: A Report of the Carnegie Foundation for the Advancement of Teaching* (New York: Harper & Row, Pub., 1983), p. 85.

[4] *Ibid.*, p. 85.

as writing."[5] The National Commission encourages "the teaching of computer science . . . in the study of the other Basics and for personal and work-related purposes."[6] Hurray, they approve of my ideas.

If word processing is the tool, we still need to develop a *method* of teaching writing with it. Then we can provide the salvation for modern education. According to two articles in the *New York Times*, "writing should be viewed not just as a way to produce a finished product but also as a learning process"[7] since "the reasoning and organizing that underlie competent writing are the foundation blocks for all subjects."[8]

Along with giving us the means to teach students to write well, word processing is an excellent way to help students acquire computer literacy. Since most students will not be programmers, but will use computers in some way, the experts on computer literacy see considerable value in word processing. Indeed, Arthur Luerhmann, in writing of the computer "survival skills" needed today, states, "Probably the most useful way to learn these things is in the context of using a computer as an aid to writing."[9]

Peter McWilliams, a popular writer whose major focus has been computers, sees word processors as "tools that serve the word processing that goes on in the ultimate word processor, the human mind."[10] Of course, the world's great philosophers haven't yet figured out just how words are processed in the human mind. So we try our best to find methods that will lead students to use their minds well. Essentially, according to the book *Writers as Teachers, Teachers as Writers*, "what one wants is to create an occasion where students can come to discovery."[11]

Perhaps the best-known leader in the teaching of writing is Donald Graves. He too sees the possibilities of word processing; "I think marvelous things can be done with the computer as a word processor—if it's in the hands of someone who really knows writing."[12] That's us! The word-processing computer is our tool, and we are its masters. After years of emphasizing math and science in schools, now it's time for English teachers to take center stage.

Among those of us who have been working with word processors in education is Colette Daiute, of Harvard, who sees that "since the computer makes it easier to

[5] *Ibid.*, p. 196.

[6] The National Commission on Excellence in Education, *A Nation At Risk*, p. 26.

[7] Nicole Simmons, "Writing Spreads Across the Curriculum," *The New York Times*, January 8, 1984, sec. 12, p. 36.

[8] Gene Maeroff, "Teaching of Writing Gets New Push," *The New York Times*, January 8, 1984, sec. 12, p. 1.

[9] Arthur Luerhmann, "The Best Way to Teach Computer Literacy," *Electronic Learning*, 3, no. 7 (April 1984), 40.

[10] Peter McWilliams, *The Word Processing Book, A Short Course in Computer Literacy* (Los Angeles: Prelude Press, 1982), p. 23.

[11] Jonathan Baumbach, *Writers As Teachers, Teachers As Writers* (New York: Holt, Rinehart & Winston, 1970), p. 5.

[12] Donald Graves, interviewed by John O. Green, "Computers, Kids, and Writing: An Interview with Donald Graves," *Classroom Computer Learning*, 4, no. 8 (March 1984), 21.

essential element of true participation in the creative process: The cursor is your pointer, yet you can never catch it. It always stays one step ahead of you."[27]

This metaphor gets at the essence not only of the creative process of writing, but also of the creative process of teaching. We attempt the best method with our students, and then derive an even better method. In all creativity, in all processes, more is always possible.

Now let's go on to the specifics of the writing process in the classroom: the modules for instruction. They are my best, for now.

[27]G. Berton Latamore, "A Fluid Well for Your Words," *Personal Computing*, 7, no. 1 January 1983), 106.

PART II
MODULES FOR CLASSROOM INSTRUCTION

INTRODUCTION: USING THE MODULES

The format used to present specific topics is that of modules, or units in lesson format. Each module can be used in its entirety or pulled apart to provide as much material as is needed. Motivation is the first part of the lesson for the students. It draws them into the work and starts the Prewriting stage. Since classroom activities flow smoothly from one writing stage to another, the entire POWER Process is contained in the Procedure section. Often, Prewriting is continued from the Motivation into the Procedure. Organizing follows logically from Prewriting; however, they are often intertwined. Writing practice, Exchanging, and Revising are often intermingled as well since exercises of each type build on one another.

Among the many activities in the book, there are some specialized pieces that can be used both in regular English classes and in special courses. For example, poetry or drama might be taught in a creative writing class or included in a more general course. Modules that deal with competency test preparation can be used during the term when the test is given. While not every state has the same examinations that New York currently administers, there is a movement in many places to begin testing for minimum competencies, and the exam modules included here may apply in part if not totally to many such tests of writing abilities.

The modules are not intended to be single-class lessons. For one thing, students differ widely in the amount of time they need to compose. In addition, prewriting activities may take ten minutes or thirty depending on the interaction in the classroom. The process of revision may consume considerable time at the beginning but become quicker later in the term. Therefore, the modules are units; they cover the topic but do not require completion in any specified time.

The first module is an introduction to word processing. Students who are familiar with the keyboard will need less practice with it than will novices. And some word processing programs require less time to learn than others. If some students are familiar with the keyboard or the software, they can help the others at the beginning. Students can learn the essential functions of the word processing program first (entering text, inserting, deleting), and move onto the advanced features when they are comfortable with what word processing is and can do. For students to use word processing for writing and to forget the mechanics in favor of thinking, they must be given an opportunity at the outset to learn the keyboard and to play with the program.

The modules for grammar appear after specific writing instruction; however, these should be integrated into the term's work as they are needed. Again, a whole module may not be necessary for each topic. Since teaching styles and types of classes vary, the modules are meant to be flexible. Use them as they are, or adapt them to fit your style or your classes.

Section I
Word Processing

MODULE 1
WORD PROCESSING: HOW AND WHY

AIM

To teach students what we do with a word processor

OBJECTIVES

By the end of this module, students will be able to

Explain what a word processor is.

Identify the components of a word-processing system.

Discuss the advantages of word processing.

Use the computer keyboard.

Recognize and use word-processing terminology.

Practice using the functions of the word processor.

MATERIALS

A passage that contains errors, stored on disk.

Note 1: To avoid making up your own passage, you may want to select one that contains errors the author placed there deliberately, such as a paragraph from *Flowers for Algernon*, by Daniel Keyes.

Note 2: The easiest way to ensure that the passage will be available for all students is to type it once on your word processor and then save it on all student file disks.

MOTIVATION

Ask students to describe the advantages and disadvantages of these three methods of transportation: horse, bicycle, and car. Elicit a statement about the improvements that technology creates.

PROCEDURE

1. Ask how a typewriter represents an improvement over pen and paper.
2. Ask students to list the disadvantages of both pens and typewriters.
3. Point out that a word processor represents an improvement over the pen and the typewriter just as the car represents an improvement over other means of land transportation.
4. Discuss what a word processor is. Explain how it represents an improvement over the typewriter.
5. Describe the equipment needed for a word processor.
   A. Hardware: computer, monitor, disk drive, printer, cables
   B. Software: word-processing program, file disk
6. Discuss differences between the typewriter and the computer keyboards.
7. *Exercise:* Load a "typing tutor" program. Students practice using the keyboard to become familiar with the QWERTY arrangement. Time should be spent in practicing "touch typing" methods.
8. Explain how we load word-processing software into the computer. Demonstrate technique. Have students load the program into their computers.
9. *Exercise:* Use and define terminology as students follow the directions below:
   A. Type your first and last name (enter text).
   B. Move the cursor five spaces forward.
   C. Move the cursor back to your last name.
   D. Delete your last name.
   E. Retype your last name.
   F. Move the cursor back to the first letter of your last name.
   G. Insert your middle name or initial and skip a space.
   H. Move the cursor to the next line.
   I. Type "hello therr."
   J. Correct the error.

10. *Practice:* Load the passage from disk. Have students correct the errors. Discuss method and results.

11. Explain that if one wanted to know how many times this passage contained the word "the," it would be possible to find out.
    A. Have students count by hand.
    B. Mention GLOBAL SEARCH function of word processor.
    C. Demonstrate use of GLOBAL SEARCH to identify each appearance of "the."

12. Explain that if one wanted to change "the" to something else, this change could readily be made on a word processor.
    A. Demonstrate GLOBAL SEARCH and REPLACE.
    B. *Exercise:* Have students search for every occurrence of the word "a" and replace it with "one."
    C. Discuss how this function could be helpful when students write.

13. Ask: If we wanted to start a new paragraph beginning with the last sentence, how would we accomplish that? Demonstrate the method and have students perform the task.

14. Ask: If we decided that this new paragraph should come before the first paragraph, what could we do?
    A. Demonstrate BLOCK MOVE.
    B. Have students exchange the two paragraphs.
    C. Have students exchange paragraphs again.
    D. Discuss how this function can be helpful to a writer.

15. Explain how to make these changes permanent. Demonstrate the procedure to save text. Use a new filename and demonstrate that by this device both versions can be stored on disk.

16. *Exercise:* Have students use a new file and type a sentence that introduces the original passage.

17. Ask students how they would put their introduction and text together into one document.
    A. Demonstrate MERGE function.
    B. Have students merge their corrected versions of the original passage with their new introductions and save the whole in a new file.
    Note: Not all word processors are capable of merging or appending files.

18. Explain that a writer has finished and wants to print what has been written (hard, or paper, copy), there is a simple procedure to follow.
    A. Have students access their print files.
    B. Demonstrate formatting. Have students format their text as you demonstrate.
    C. Have students print their documents.

19. Explain what students should do when they discover an error or something they don't like.
    A. Discuss editing on the screen and printing another copy.

    B. *Exercise:* Demonstrate embedding format lines in the text. Have students center a title with an embedded command.

    C. Have students print another copy and save the change they have made on disk.

20. *Practice:* Have students spend time using the functions of the word processor. Note: See Additional Activities for suggestions of texts they can use for practice.

SUMMARY

Review all that word processing can do for us.

ADDITIONAL ACTIVITIES

1. *Literature:* Any of the following can be entered on a word processor for practice:
    A. Plot summary
    B. Character analysis and/or description
    C. Letter to a character
    D. Response of any type to a situation from class literature

2. *Vocabulary:* Students can use class vocabulary to create sentences and paragraphs on the word processor.

3. *Media:* Students can write any of the following on the word processor:
    A. Letter to the editor
    B. Advice to a TV character
    C. Movie or TV show review

Section II
Processing Words

MODULE 2
SENTENCE COMBINING

AIM

To teach students to write concise sentences and to vary the sentences they use.

OBJECTIVES

By the end of this module, students will be able to

Demonstrate sentence variety.
Demonstrate sentence conciseness.
Combine sentences for effective expression.

MATERIALS

An exercise stored on disk. See Notes.

MOTIVATION

Begin by asking students to type two sentences that tell about something they did yesterday.

PROCEDURE

1. Tell students to use their word processors to combine the two sentences into one. They should be careful; the resulting sentence must be correct.
2. Ask students how they joined two ideas in a single sentence. (Analyze the process of sentence combining.)
3. Discuss methods used to combine sentences:
   A. Adding and subtracting words. Load Exercise 1 from disk. Have students add and subtract words to create one effective sentence.
   B. Changing the form of words. Load Exercise 2 from disk. Have students add, subtract, and change the form of words—for example, changing "ticked" to "ticking."
   C. Adding groups of words. Load Exercise 3 from disk. Have students combine groups of words—phrases and clauses—to create complex sentences. (A finished sentence might begin, "Adelaide, who is a sports-minded ant, came to our . . . .")

   After completing this exercise, and those that preceded it, students can work with partners to revise their answers.
4. *Practice:*
   A. Have students load Exercise 4 from disk and create the most concise two sentences they can. Afterwards, they can discuss and revise their sentences with a partner.
   B. Have students work in pairs, with one partner creating a series of sentences and the second partner trying to combine them.
5. Discuss combining sentence elements in a way that shows relationships.
   A. Load Exercise 5 from disk and discuss how to combine groups of words to show each of the following relationships:
      1. who
      2. which or that
      3. when
      4. where
   B. Have students practice creating sentences that show these relationships.
   C. Let students discuss and revise their results with a partner.
6. Discuss combining clauses to create complex sentences which show relationships.
   A. Load Exercise 6 from disk and discuss how to combine groups of words to create complex sentences that show the following relationships:
      1. cause and effect
      2. sequence
      3. condition
      4. contrast
   B. For each example, have students list other words that express the same relationship in different sentences.

C. Let students practice creating complex sentences that show the four different relationships.
D. Have students discuss and revise results with a partner.
7. *Exercise:* Tell students to write a paragraph, then to combine some of the sentences. They should discuss and revise their paragraphs with a partner.

SUMMARY

Review the reasons and the best methods for combining sentences.

Activity

Have each student load a passage he or she created for the additional activities section of Module 1 and use sentence-combining techniques to improve the passage.

ADDITIONAL ACTIVITIES

1. *Literature:* Have students create a story line that summarizes the plot of whatever literature the class is reading. The students can then create a variety of sentences from the story line by using sentence-combining methods.
2. *Vocabulary:* Using a class vocabulary list stored on disk, students can write a simple sentence for each word. They can then use sentence-combining methods to create varied sentences.
3. *Media:*
    A. Have students use sentence combining to rewrite a news article.
    B. Have students use TV program listings and combine the review blurbs for two shows to create a sentence.

NOTES

Sentence-combining exercises

1. Morris is a small, ugly muskrat.
    He took a spider from its web.
    He used it as chewing gum.
2. The clock got on my nerves.
    It ticked loudly.
3. Adelaide is a sports-minded ant.
    She came to our picnic.
    She swam in the soup.
    Adelaide also ran track around a slice of bread.

4. Reginald is an octopus.
   Reginald and a mermaid are friends.
   He visits the mermaid's cave and brings flowers.
   They swim in the ocean hand in hand in hand in hand. . . .

5. *Group 1:*
   Henry is a silly-looking hyena.
   He likes to laugh a lot.

   Group 2:
   Henry saw a bicycle outside his cage.
   He thought it was silly-looking.

   Group 3:
   Henry looked and looked at the bike.
   He started to laugh like a hyena.

   Group 4:
   Henry likes living in the zoo.
   So many silly-looking things and people pass by his cage.

6. *Group 1:*
   Timothy is a toad.
   People think he has warts.

   Group 2:
   The chicken chicken ran away.
   The farmer walked into the barn with an axe.

   Group 3:
   There are six more weeks of winter.
   The groundhog saw his shadow.

   Group 4:
   Samuel is a spider.
   He is not a creep.

MODULE 3
PROOFREADING AND REVISING

AIM

To teach students ways to make sure their written work is correct.

OBJECTIVES

By the end of this module, students will be able to

> Identify and correct errors in grammar, usage, and thought.
> Use the word processor to proofread and revise.

MATERIALS

A passage containing errors, stored on disk as in Module 1.

MOTIVATION

Begin by asking the students what we use grammar and punctuation for.

PROCEDURE

1. Review common grammatical concepts or aspects of usage that you have found your students need to review. Note: If extensive review is necessary, use the modules in Section VII.
2. *Review:* Ask students how we use a word processor to correct our mistakes. Discuss various editing functions, such as INSERT, DELETE, and BLOCK MOVES.
3. Ask students what other usage details we can check for when we proofread. (They should mention indenting for paragraphs, spelling, word use, etc.)
4. *Exercise:* Load passage from disk. Have students correct the errors and discuss their corrections.
5. Ask students why correcting our own errors is more difficult than correcting someone else's.

6. Discuss methods to use in checking for errors.
   A. Separate writing and proofreading by enough time so the work can be seen fresh.
   B. Read passage from the bottom up to find errors of usage or grammar.
   C. Check one sentence at a time and correct.
   D. Read paragraphs as individual entities.
   E. Reread from top to bottom for flow of ideas.
7. *Practice:* Have students load a brief passage they created for the Additional Activities in Module 1 and proofread their work. They should check their work with a partner.
8. Discuss the difference between proofreading and revising.
9. Ask how a word processor can be used to revise what we write. Describe the stages of revision:
   A. Enter text on word processor and save on disk.
   B. Print out hard copy.
   C. Reread for unity, coherence, creativity, etc. Think through ideas.
   D. Make changes on hard copy.
   E. Return to the computer to enter and save changes.
   F. Print out a second draft.
   G. Work with a co-editor or editorial group for additional improvements. Make changes on hard copy.
   H. Enter changes and save on disk; print out draft.
   I. Reread draft and rethink topic. Perform final revisions on hard copy.
   J. Enter changes and proofread for errors. Save on disk and print out copy for submission.
11. *Exercise:* Have students revise the passage used for proofreading, or load another passage they have created. They should follow the procedure outlined above to revise.

SUMMARY

Review the definitions of proofreading and revising and emphasize the importance of each.

NOTES:

Time frame

1. Students should meet with peer editorial groups to analyze and revise work throughout the year. In addition, they should continue the process of revising on hard copy at home for all assignments and enter changes on the word processor during succeeding class sessions.

2. Allow time for individual and group revising, proofreading, and entering of changes for *all* pieces of work over the course of the year.

3. To handle limited numbers of computers and/or limited access to computers, stagger assignments and utilize editorial group work.

Section III
The Craft of Writing

MODULE 4
DESCRIPTION

AIM

To develop students' abilities to describe people, places, and things.

OBJECTIVES

By the end of this module, students will be able to

Use specific detail.
Describe characters.
Create setting and atmosphere.
Find topics for writing.
Begin a journal.

MATERIALS

Exercises stored on disk. See Notes.

MOTIVATION

Tell students to close their eyes and picture something, then open their eyes and type words or phrases that describe what they saw.

PROCEDURE

1. *Guessing game:* Have students read aloud what they've written without telling what object is being described. The class will guess.
2. Ask students how a writer can re-create something so that a reader can picture it. (Use details; appeal to senses.)
3. *Exercise:* Use of detail. Load exercise from disk. Have class take general items, make them specific, and then make them detailed. Class discusses samples, then each student creates own examples.
4. *Practice:* Have students use the example of a person developed in the exercise above and create an extended image of him or her. Discuss and revise in groups.
5. *Teacher's image:* I pictured a little girl in a white pinafore. Her hair is in lots of little braids with different colored ribbons. There are matching ribbons running through the eyelets of her dress. She's wearing white nylon socks and white patent leather shoes, and she's running on an open field in Central Park; the grass is bright green because it is spring. In front of her is a mud puddle. Ask: How did I change the image with the last sentence?
6. Ask students how setting and atmosphere affect what we write. Discuss settings from a bright, sunny day to a dark, moonless night.
7. *Practice:* Have students insert setting and atmosphere into the description of a person created in Item 4. Discuss in groups to see effect and to revise work.
8. Ask class where we get ideas and subjects to write about.
   A. Observation (e.g., see a child falling on the sidewalk.)
   B. Experience (e.g., visit a new part of the city.)
   C. Printed material (e.g., advertisement: FOR SALE: lace wedding gown, size 9, never worn.)
9. Ask: When we come across anything of interest, what should we do? (Elicit the response that we should write down our ideas.)
   Exercise: Have students list ideas and subjects that could be used in their own writing.
10. Discuss journal writing—student compilation of their own writing throughout the term to explore ideas, experiences, feelings.
11. *Practice:* Have students select something from their own examples for Item 9 and write a brief description and setting. Discuss and revise in groups.

SUMMARY

Review different topics for writing and sources students can consult for ideas.

ADDITIONAL ACTIVITIES

1. *Literature:* A descriptive passage from the literature the class is reading can be stored on disk and analyzed. Students can take the character or setting and change it to see the effect.
2. *Vocabulary:* Class vocabulary list can be stored on disk. Students use words to create descriptions.
3. *Media:* Students can use headlines from the newspaper and create their own descriptions and settings or use a news story and invent description and setting for it.

NOTES

Exercise for Item 3 (Use of detail)

GENERAL	SPECIFIC	DETAILED
dog	white poodle	small white poodle with sad brown eyes
child	2-year old girl	smiling toddler in a crisp, white pinafore
street		
book		
person you know		

MODULE 5
CHARACTERIZATION

AIM

To show students how to create believable people when they write.

OBJECTIVES

By the end of this module, students will be able to

    Create passages employing personification.
    Evoke emotion and mood.
    Create characters who are believable.
    Create actions that are believable.

MATERIALS

Exercise stored on disk. See Notes.

MOTIVATION

Begin by saying, "Pretend you are a pineapple. How do you look? What happens to you when someone wants a piece of you? How do you feel?"

PROCEDURE

1. Ask students to discuss how we bring out an object's feelings.
2. *Practice:* Have students select an object, pretend they are that object, and write a brief passage to describe themselves and how they feel. Possible objects include a door, a pen, a turkey on Thanksgiving, a cactus.
3. Have students discuss their passages in groups and revise.
4. Ask students to name some emotions that people feel (e.g., love, hate, anger, sadness, happiness).
5. Discuss ways to create emotions in writing:
   A. Mood—the setting of a story.
   B. Motivation—hints about what makes a person act.

6. *Exercise:* For each emotion listed on disk, have students describe a setting that would create the right mood and then explain what action they would expect to grow out of this setting.

7. Use student examples to discuss how mood is created by setting and how actions must be motivated for characterization. (Note: The most realistic emotions we can write about are ones we have felt.)

8. *Exercise:* Have students select one situation from the list on disk and do the following:

   A. Describe the person.
   B. Create the setting (mood, atmosphere).
   C. Explain what motivated the action.

9. Have students work in groups to discuss how convincing their results are and to revise their work.

SUMMARY

Review techniques we can use to make our writing seem real.

ADDITIONAL ACTIVITIES

1. *Literature:* Select a passage from the literature the class is reading and discuss how the writer handles characterization.

2. *Vocabulary:* Use vocabulary lists to create sentences that show emotion, description, or motivation.

3. *Media:* Select a newspaper story. Expand the story to include mood and characterization.

NOTES

Exercise for Item 6 (Mood and motivation)

EMOTION	SETTING	ACTION
love	beach	kiss
hate		
anger		
fear		
joy		

Exercise for Item 8.

1. A child runs home crying.
2. A girl slaps a boy.
3. A boy runs away from home.

MODULE 6
POINT OF VIEW

AIM

To help students recognize the devices that make a story seem real.

OBJECTIVES

By the end of this module, students will be able to

Discern and use different points of view.
List the basic elements of a story.
Create a story line.

MATERIALS

Exercises on disk. See Notes.

MOTIVATION

Have students pretend that they are in a park. Say: In front of you is a puddle. What will you do about the puddle? Why?

PROCEDURE

1. Tell students they are still in the park with the puddle. Ask how they would feel about the puddle if they were
    A. A little boy
    B. The boy's mother

      C. A football player on crutches

      D. A nature lover

2. Discuss point of view, explaining that though we can all see the same thing, we may see it differently.

3. Explain that when we write a story, how we present material depends on who the character is and how much he knows. Discuss the three most common narrative points of view:

      A. First person. The narrator is a character in the story who can reveal only his thoughts and feelings and what he sees and is told by other characters.

      B. Third person objective. The narrator is an outsider who can report only what he sees and hears.

      C. Omniscient author. The narrator is an all-knowing outsider who can enter the minds of one or all of the characters.

4. *Exercise:* Load nursery rhyme from disk. Students should use first person narration to write an account of the event described in the poem from the perspective of ONE of the participants (the cat, Johnny, or Tommy).

5. Discuss passages in groups and revise.

6. Explain that when we create a story, we have to know the answers to certain questions in advance. In groups, students should discuss the following questions in terms of the stories they just wrote.
WHO? WHAT? WHERE? WHEN? WHY? HOW?

7. Tell students to take the information they have just assembled and create a story line, or outline of the situation. Explain that every story has a beginning, middle, and end, and we can use a time line to see how the story works.

beginning	middle	end
describe situation	crisis	summing up

8. Ask how the time line differs depending upon whether the point of view is that of the cat, Johnny, or Tommy.

9. *Practice:* Students select a situation, answer the questions, and fill in a time line. Then they should write a passage that creates the setting and characterization for their story. For suggested topics, students can return to items in a previous lesson or invent their own (e.g., a child runs home crying; a girl slaps a boy; a boy runs away from home).

10. Have student groups discuss results and revise.

SUMMARY

Review what we must know before we begin to write.

ADDITIONAL ACTIVITIES

1. *Literature:* Students can analyze class literature in terms of the elements discussed. They can also create a passage that tells the story from another character's point of view.
2. *Vocabulary:* Students can use vocabulary lists to create sentences for their passages.
3. *Media:* Students can use a newspaper story, analyze it in terms of the elements discussed, and write a sequel.

NOTES

Exercise for Item 4 (Nursery rhyme)

Ding, dong, bell.
The cat's in the well.
Who put her in?
Little Johnny Green.
Who pulled her out?
Little Tommy Trout.

MODULE 7
PLOT DEVELOPMENT

AIM

To teach techniques that help writing flow smoothly from beginning to end.

OBJECTIVES

By the end of this module, students will be able to

Create believable action that furthers the story line.

Begin writing with an interesting opening.

Create conflict.

Produce realistic dialogue.

NOTE: Students can use the letters A, B, C, D to remind themselves of the elements of plot development: action, beginning, conflict, dialogue.

MATERIALS

Exercises on disk. See Notes.

MOTIVATION

Discuss student responses to Item 9 in the previous module: the time line of a story.

PROCEDURE

1. Show students how to change time line into a diagram.

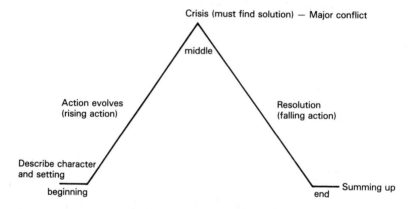

Note that action moves the story along. Action (and reaction) must be realistic to be believable in writing. (Have students decide what they would do in the character's situation.)

2. *Exercise:* Load the two situations from disk. Discuss which is outwardly more realistic and how the other could be introduced in a way that would make it more believable.

3. Discuss: How much of what we write is based on ourselves?

4. Discuss ways to begin stories.
   A. Start with an eye-catching opener.
   B. Create setting and atmosphere.
   C. Introduce character. (Describe the character and demonstrate elements of characterization.)

5. *Exercise:* Have students list the items they would use to begin the story of Joe or Bob. Discuss in groups.

6. *Practice:* Load the passage students created in response to Item 9 in previous lesson (also used in motivation today). Students should add an eye-catching opening and revise text to conform with items B and C above. Discuss results in groups and revise.

7. Most of the time the crisis (high point of the diagram) is a conflict of some type. Discuss the possible kinds of conflict:
   A. One person against another person.
   B. A person against himself.
   C. A person against society (rules, etc.).
8. Ask how our stories about Joe or Bob can fit any one of these conflict patterns.
9. *Exercise:* Tell students to decide which conflict they would use for the story they have been working on. Discuss results in groups and revise.
10. When there is action (and reaction), there is speech. Ask students how they can create believable dialogue:
    A. KISS—Keep It Short and Sweet. Real people speak in phrases and sentences, not in paragraphs.
    B. Write what *you* would say in the character's situation.
11. *Exercise:* Have students write two sentences that Joe or Bob might say. Use quotation marks as if the sentences were pieces of the story. Discuss results in groups and revise.
12. *Practice:* Have students write dialogue between two characters in the story they have been working on. Discuss results in groups and revise.

SUMMARY

Review techniques that can help move a story from beginning to end.

ADDITIONAL ACTIVITIES

1. *Literature:* Analyze literature class reading in terms of action, beginning, conflict, and dialogue. Students can list these elements for plot summaries.
2. *Vocabulary:* Students can use class vocabulary lists in action or dialogue sentences or in a story line.
3. *Media:* Students can review a TV program in terms of action, beginning, conflict, and dialogue.

NOTES

Situations

1. Joe got a failing mark in science on his report card, so he hid the card from his mother.
2. Bob got a failing mark in science on his report card, so he jumped out of a window.

Section IV
The Forms of Writing

```
+-----------------------------------------------------+
|                                                     |
|                    MODULE 8                         |
|                    NARRATIVE                         |
|                                                     |
+-----------------------------------------------------+
```

AIM

To introduce different ways of telling a story.

OBJECTIVES

By the end of this module, students will be able to

    Create fantasy.
    Create all elements of a narrative.
    Create a story line.
    Explain technical devices.
    Put all elements together to produce a story.

MATERIALS

Exercise stored on disk. See Notes.

MOTIVATION

Ask students what would happen if they were home alone, lying in bed, and heard very strange noises.

PROCEDURE

1. Ask students what they must decide first in order to write a story about this situation. Have them work as a class or in small groups to plan the WHO, WHAT, WHERE, WHEN, WHY, and HOW of their story. They should indicate a type of conflict and provide plans for characterization as well as a diagram of plot.
2. Discuss results. So far we have almost all of the elements for a story:
   A. Setting
   B. Characterization
   C. Plot (including conflict)
3. Ask what might be a good opening sentence and title for this story.
4. This story is an example of fantasy. What other types of stories are considered fantasy? (Fables, mysteries, occult stories, horror stories, monster stories.) What is the purpose of fantasy?
5. In any of these fantasy stories, the element of suspense is even more evident than in other narratives.
   Discuss ways to create suspense.
6. Ask: If it were possible that something strange could be outside the door, what could we do to our story to get readers to believe it?
   A. Use foreshadowing—the art of hinting so you prepare the reader for what will happen.
   B. Create real people and a real place so readers will suspend disbelief when a strange thing happens.
7. *Exercise:* Load items for sequencing from disk. Have students put them in order and discuss reasons for the chosen order in groups.
8. *Exercise:* Have students insert other elements of plot (foreshadowing, climax, resolution) into list and discuss results in groups.
9. Tell students they are going to create their own original narratives. Discuss places to look for ideas (e.g., own journals, overheard conversations, photographs, news pictures, news story, Dear Abby column, a personal experience that's raised a value question, a scene observed, or an interesting person encountered recently).
10. *Practice:* Have students select an idea and develop a story line. They add other narrative elements as mentioned above to form notes. Then they create the story.

11. Students work in groups to revise stories.
12. OPTIONAL: Discuss some writers' tricks.
    A. Irony—a contradiction between what is said and what is meant or between what the character thinks is true and what the reader knows is true.
    B. Satire—exaggeration that makes fun of someone or something.
    C. Humor—funny situation or speech.
    Note: All three of these effects are difficult to create. Examples from literature can be used to demonstrate appropriate techniques.

SUMMARY

Review ways to write an effective story.

ADDITIONAL ACTIVITIES

1. *Literature:* Students analyze a story from class literature in terms of narrative elements.
2. *Vocabulary:* Students use class vocabulary in their journals or narratives.
3. *Media:* Students create story line and narrative for one episode of an original soap opera or sitcom.

NOTES

Story items for sequencing

1. The jewelry box was under the bed.
2. The hotel room had been cleaned.
3. Mary's gold necklace was missing.
4. The detective visited the scene of the crime.
5. The short, blond maid was wearing a gold necklace.

MODULE 9
EXPOSITION

AIM

To demonstrate ways to explain something in writing.

OBJECTIVES

By the end of this module, students will be able to

Use traditional paragraph form.

Write a paragraph that gives reasons, examples, or illustrations.

Write a paragraph that compares or contrasts.

Write a paragraph that shows cause and effect.

MATERIALS

Exercises on disk. See Notes.

MOTIVATION

Ask two students to volunteer to do the following: One student explains how to do something (e.g., tie a shoelace, draw a stick figure) step by step. The other student follows these directions precisely to see how accurate they are.

PROCEDURE

1. Ask: How difficult is it to explain how to do something? What must we do in order to explain ourselves well?
2. Ask students how they could explain the sentence below:
   "There is a type of weather to suit any of my moods."
   A. Discuss giving reasons, examples, or illustrations.
   B. Discuss form of paragraph: topic sentence, reasons, summary or clincher sentence.
   C. Create a model paragraph with the class.

3. Mention that when we write explanations of this type, transitional phrases (e.g., "in the first place," "for example," "furthermore") can often help us.

4. *Exercise:* Have students select a sentence from examples on disk and develop a paragraph using reasons, examples, or illustrations.

5. Have students form groups to compare ideas and techniques and to revise work.

6. Ask students how they would explain the sentence below:
    "It is more fun to be a guest than a host."
    A. Discuss comparison and contrast.
    B. Discuss form of paragraph: topic sentence, comparison or contrast, summary or clincher sentence.
    C. Create a model paragraph with the class.

7. Mention transitional expressions (e.g., "but," "on the other hand," "however,") that can be used for comparison or contrast.

8. *Exercise:* Students select a sentence from the examples on disk and develop a paragraph by comparing or contrasting.

9. Students form groups based on sentences selected to compare ideas and techniques and to revise work.

10. Ask students how they could explain the sentence below:
    "Many people drink poison by mistake."
    A. Discuss cause and effect.
    B. Discuss paragraph form: topic sentence, cause and effect, clincher sentence.
    C. Create a model paragraph with the class.

11. Mention transitional expressions (e.g., "therefore", "for this reason," "as a result," "so") that can be used to show cause and effect.

12. *Exercise:* Have students select from sentences on disk and develop a paragraph by showing cause and effect.

13. Students form groups to compare ideas and technique and to revise work.

14. *Practice:* Students select one of the topics they have used and develop their ideas into several paragraphs.

15. Students work in groups to revise.

SUMMARY

Review methods that can be used to explain ideas in writing.

ADDITIONAL ACTIVITIES

1. *Literature:* Students analyze passages of explanation from class literature.

2. *Vocabulary:* Students integrate vocabulary into expository writing.
3. *Media:* Students analyze newspaper articles and columns in terms of expository technique.

NOTES

Sentences for Item 4 (Reasons, examples, illustrations)

1. Actions speak louder than words.
2. Everyone should give to some charity.
3. My favorite subject is _ _ _ _ _ _.

Sentences for Item 8 (Comparison, contrast)

1. There is a vast difference between an apartment and a house.
2. Girls/Boys are better at _ _ _ _ _ _ than boys/girls.
3. The city is better than the country.

Sentences for Item 12 (Cause and effect)

1. Weather often causes damage.
2. There are superstitions that work.
3. It pays to study.

MODULE 10
AUTOBIOGRAPHY

AIM

To help students write about themselves.

OBJECTIVES

By the end of this module, students will be able to

>   Explore thoughts and ideas in writing.
>   Present a written picture of themselves.
>   Write an autobiography.

MATERIALS

Exercise stored on disk. See Notes.

MOTIVATION

Load topics from disk. Discuss what they mean and the purpose of thinking or writing about them.

PROCEDURE

1. Each student must select five items from those listed on the disk and write journal entries for them.
2. Ask: What kinds of things have you learned from writing these journal entries?
3. Have students write a journal entry about what their lives will be like ten years from now.
4. Discuss students' views of their future.
5. Have students write a journal entry about what they plan to do between now and ten years from now so their futures will be what they want.
6. Discuss cause and effect as it relates to the students' lives.
7. Have students write two journal entries:
   A. How I see myself
   B. How others see me
8. Discuss differences in points of view and how we want to portray ourselves in writing.
9. Discuss selecting items from the past that fit into a sequence for the future.
10. Have students write a journal entry about what they have done with their lives so far to lead to the futures they want.
11. Have students add factual and descriptive material and use the journal entries to help them write autobiographies.

SUMMARY

Review ways we have to portray ourselves in writing.

ADDITIONAL ACTIVITIES

1. *Literature:* Choose autobiographical passages from class literature and discuss in terms of selecting a portrait the author wants to present.

2. *Vocabulary:* Students integrate vocabulary into journal entries and auto-biography.

3. *Media:* Students read newspaper profiles to see how a person is portrayed and discuss how a person presents a particular image.

NOTES

Topics for Motivation

1. A gift I would like to give
2. A gift I would like to receive
3. My pet peeve
4. An object I cherish
5. An opinion I hold
6. A trait I approve of
7. A trait I dislike
8. Something I learned
9. Friendship
10. My favorite relative

MODULE 11
POETRY

AIM

To teach techniques useful for writing poetry.

OBJECTIVES

By the end of this module, students will be able to

Create poetic images.

Use sound and rhythm patterns.

Use poetic devices.

Use various poetic forms.

Produce a classroom poetry magazine.

Create greeting cards.

MATERIALS

Exercises on disk. See Notes.

MOTIVATION

Ask students what beauty is. Discuss ways to express abstract ideas. Elicit other abstract ideas (e.g., happiness, sadness, ugliness, hope, fear, anger).

PROCEDURE

1. Ask students to find some concrete examples (images) that express the abstract idea of sadness.
   A. Have students type "Sadness" as a title.
   B. Tell them to list images (each on a separate line).
   C. Urge use of detail for each example (e.g., a tearful child, a homeless old man).
2. Have students decide what tone/mood this list should convey and delete the items that don't really help to convey it.
3. Review method of expanding detail discussed in Module 4. Expand one of the images with the class (e.g., A homeless old man leaning on his cane trudges down Broadway).
4. Explain that we can expand the other images and then use BLOCK MOVES to rearrange the order of our list to create the best effect. The result is a mini-poem on sadness. Work with class to create mini-poem.
5. We can expand one of our images even more to create a single poem. (Ask: Who is this old man? Where is he going? Can you describe him more thoroughly?) Elicit lines from the class.
6. *Practice:* Have students select another abstract idea and use the procedure above to create their own image poems. Groups evaluate and revise poems.
7. Ask: What is your favorite color? Why?
8. Discuss how a color can be the topic of a poem.
9. *Practice:* Type the name of your color as a title and use the abstract-idea procedure to create a poem. Groups evaluate and revise poems.
10. Discuss other ideas that could be the topics for poems. (Elicit ideas such as seasons, five senses.)
11. *Practice:* Have students select one example from each group listed in Item 10 and create poems. Groups evaluate and revise poems.
12. Lyrics to songs are often considered poetry. What features of poetry are more obvious in lyrics? (Note: A popular song can be played and the lyrics stored on disk for analysis.)

A. Rhythm—pattern of accented and unaccented syllables.
  1. Read some student work (from above) aloud to listen to rhythm.
  2. Have groups revise own poems to create internal rhythm.
B. Sound Patterns. Poems that demonstrate each of the following can be stored on disk for analysis.
  1. Alliteration—repetition of initial sounds (e.g., "angry alligator")
  2. Assonance—repetition of vowel sounds (e.g., "bright light")
  3. Consonance—repetition of consonant sounds (e.g., "I wanna banana")
  4. Onomatopoeia—words that sound like what they mean (e.g., "crack," "hiss")
  5. Rhyme—repetition of sounds at the end of lines.

13. *Exercise:* Load poem from disk. Have students identify the sound patterns. Then have them construct examples of each sound pattern using the words given in the second part of the exercise. Discuss when to use (not overuse) sound patterns.

14. *Practice:* Have student groups review their poems to see if they have included any sound devices. They may revise where the insertion of sound pattern produces a more effective poem.

15. There are poetic devices that are visually descriptive rather than sound oriented. What are these?
  A. Simile—comparison using "like" or "as" (e.g., "sly as a fox")
  B. Metaphor—implied comparison (e.g., "That boy is a clown.")
  C. Hyperbole—exaggeration to make a point (e.g., "I could have danced all night.")

16. *Exercise:* Load completion exercise from disk. Have students do the work and discuss results in groups.

17. *Practice:* Student groups review their poems to see if they have included any of these poetic devices. They may revise where the use of these devices improves the effect of their poems.

18. Poems can be written in traditional or unusual forms. Discuss the following forms. Have students experiment with them.
  A. Haiku—a three-line, unrhymed poem with five syllables in the first line, seven in the second, and five in the third. It usually presents an image.
  B. Limerick—a five-line, rhymed poem with the first, second, and last lines rhymed and with no more than nine syllables each. The third and fourth lines are rhymed and have no more than six syllables each.
  C. Shaped verse—an unrhymed poem in which the shape or form explains what the poem is about.

SUMMARY

Review definition of a poem and the purposes poems serve.

SUMMARY ACTIVITIES

1. *Classroom magazine:* You can use the MERGE function of the word processor to print several student works on the same page. In this way you can compile a classroom mini-magazine.
2. *Class project:* Students can create poetic greeting cards for their own use or (if artwork can be added) for sale as a fund raiser.

ADDITIONAL ACTIVITIES

1. *Literature:* Use class literature to demonstrate many of the techniques discussed in this lesson. Students can imitate the style of various poets.
2. *Vocabulary:* Class vocabulary can be used in poems or exercises.
3. *Media:* Students can look for poems in magazines. They can also create poems about news events or people in the news.

NOTES

Exercises for Item 13

SOUND PATTERNS

Little Miss Muffet
Sat on her tuffet
Eating her curds and whey.
Along came a spider
And sat down beside her
And frightened Miss Muffet away.

STUDENT SOUND PATTERNS

Alliteration:

1. Breeze
2. Summer
3. Sea

Assonance:

1. Rain
2. Book
3. Picnic

Consonance:

1. Picture
2. Animal
3. Cart

Onomatopoeia:

1.
2.
3.

Rhyme:

1. _ _ _ _ _ _ and _ _ _ _ _ _
2. _ _ _ _ _ _ and _ _ _ _ _ _
3. _ _ _ _ _ _ and _ _ _ _ _ _

Exercise for Item 16 (poetic devices)

Simile: Complete the phrases:

1. Quick as _ _ _ _ _ _
2. Frightened as _ _ _ _ _ _
3. Clever as _ _ _ _ _ _
4. Hair like _ _ _ _ _ _
5. Cheeks like _ _ _ _ _ _

Metaphor: Write an implied comparison for the following:

1. A snowflake
2. An abandoned building
3. A tree

Hyperbole: Write a statement about each of the following items and exaggerate to make a point:

1. Hunger
2. Overweight
3. Pain

MODULE 12
DRAMA

AIM

To teach students what makes a play a play.

OBJECTIVES

By the end of this module, students will be able to

Format dramatic sketches.

Enter stage directions, dramatic dialogue, and dramatic structure.

Create a dramatic script.

Edit a script to heighten dramatic effect.

MATERIALS

Exercises to be stored on disk. See Notes.

MOTIVATION

Say: You are on a subway train and hear X make the following statement: "I can't find my money." Load the statement from disk and write Y's reply.

PROCEDURE

1. Discuss the responses to the motivation.
    A. What types of responses are most effective? Why?
    B. How is dramatic dialogue different from narrative dialogue?
    C. How do we create effective dialogue?
        1. Lines must fit character.
        2. Lines should sound like real conversation.
        3. Lines should be short.
2. Ask how playwrights indicate movement and visual effects (by stage direc-

tions). Discuss how stage directions are used in a sketch such as the one above to indicate each of the following:

   A. Entrances and exits

   B. General physical movement

   C. Manner of saying a line

   D. Physical indications of emotions

3. What elements of narrative are used in writing plays? (Setting, characterization, plot.)

4. *Setting:*

   A. How is the setting the same in narrative and in drama?

   B. How is it different?

   C. *Exercise:* Students write and insert setting and stage directions for the sketch from Motivation. They discuss and revise results in groups.

5. *Characterization:*

   A. How is characterization the same in narrative and drama?

   B. How is it different?

   C. *Exercise:* Students write notes about characterization. At this point they should add one more line for each character.

   D. Use GLOBAL SEARCH and REPLACE to give characters X and Y real names.

   E. Student groups evaluate and revise results.

6. *Plot:*

   A. How is plot development the same in narrative and in drama?

   B. How is it different?

   C. *Exercise:* Students add more dialogue that leads into the plot development of the sketch. They discuss results in groups.

   D. How do we show conflict?

   E. How do we resolve the conflict and show resolution?

   F. Students discuss how conflict could be shown in their sketches.

7. *Exercise:* Load situations from disk.

   A. Students select one and write the setting and opening lines (with stage directions).

   B. Students indicate (in note form) the characterization of their main characters and (in diagram form) the plot development (include climax and resolution).

   C. Groups discuss development of the short plays.

8. *Practice:*

   A. Students return to word processor to create a scene.

   B. Students' editorial groups meet to revise and suggest ideas for next scene.

   C. Repeat A and B until scripts have been completed and revised.

   D. Scripts should be performed (or read aloud) to see dramatic effect.

SUMMARY

Review ways of writing effective drama.

ADDITIONAL ACTIVITIES

1. *Literature:* Dramatic scenes from class literature can be used for analysis. Also, passages can be rewritten in dramatic form.
2. *Vocabulary:* Students integrate class vocabulary into their sketches.
3. *Media:* Students analyze situation comedy or made-for-TV drama and write a sequel.

NOTES

Exercise for motivation

X: I can't find my money!
Y:

Exercise for Item 7 (Situations)

GENERAL

1. A lie
2. An accusation
3. Stealing
4. Doing domething impulsive
5. A fight

SPECIFIC

1. One friend wants to steal something in a department store.
2. Someone wants to leave a party but his or her ride has had too much to drink.
3. A boy wants to ask a certain girl out. (Or a girl wants to ask a certain boy out.)
4. Someone promised to clean his or her room, but his or her friends are going to a good movie.
5. Two friends are walking on a lonely, deserted street at night.

MODULE 13
JOURNALISM

AIM

To introduce students to newspaper writing.

OBJECTIVES

By the end of this module, students will be able to

Use the inverted pyramid.
Enter and edit a news story.
Create and insert headlines.
Write a feature article.
Compose an editorial.

MATERIALS

News story from daily paper and additional newspapers.

MOTIVATION

Ask students what they think it means to have a "nose for news."

PROCEDURE

1. What is news? (News formula: event + people + interest to readers.)
2. Ask how and where we can find news. Discuss each of the following:
   A. Being on the lookout for events and details.
   B. Beats—locations where news is likely.
   C. Kinds of stories—advance, spot news, follow-up, continuing.
3. Ask how we gather information.
4. Ask what information we need (who?, what?, where?, when?, why?, how?).
5. Newspapers have their own vocabulary. Define and discuss: *lead, byline, headline, masthead, dateline, wire service, top story*.

6. Consider how we write a news story once we have all the information:
   A. Lead paragraph— a summary, which begins with climactic event or statement of meaning.
   B. Answers to the questions Who?, What?, Where?, etc.
   C. Inverted pyramid—form and use.

7. *Exercise:* Select a current news story and reproduce it for the entire class or store it on disk.
   A. Discuss lead, answers to Who?, What?, etc., and inverted pyramid.
   B. Discuss headlines and subheads—purpose and how created.
   C. Rewrite a fairy tale (e.g., Goldilocks) as a news story with the whole class.

8. *Exercise:* Have students work on one of the story items listed on disk.
   A. Create answers to Who?, What?, etc., and write the lead, additional paragraphs, and a headline.
   B. Student groups print out, analyze, and revise their work.

9. Discuss styles of various newspapers: *New York Times, Washington Post, National Enquirer, USA Today*, local newspaper.

10. Issues for discussion:
    A. The ethics of journalism
    B. How the media create news

11. Discuss how feature articles are different from news.
    A. News peg—tied to an event, not the event itself
    B. Time copy—not related to an event
    C. Form and length—regular feature, sidebar

12. Discuss the purposes of features: to entertain, inform, expand knowledge.

13. Discuss the types of feature articles:
    A. Human-interest
    B. Personality sketches
    C. Historical features
    D. How-to
    E. Analysis of a problem

14. *Exercise:*
    A. Have students locate an example of each type of feature for analysis.
    B. Fairy tale used in Item 7 can be used again to demonstrate various types of feature articles.

15. *Exercises:*
    A. Students select a news peg from school event or earlier work and write a brief feature article that could be run as a sidebar. Groups analyze and revise copy.
    B. Students gather information on a time-copy article of their own choice and write the article. Groups print out, analyze, and revise copy.

16. Some features take the form of columns on certain types of information. What are some examples?
    A. Reviews—of books, films, TV shows, plays
    B. Columns on topical issues—home, food, science, business, science, sports, etc.

17. *Exercises:*
    A. Students select reviews and topical columns for analysis in small groups.
    B. Students work with fairy tale used earlier to demonstrate the slant of a column.
    C. Groups print out, edit, and revise.

18. *Practice:*
    A. Students select a book, TV show, etc., and write a review. Groups analyze and revise work.
    B. Students select a topical issue and write a column. Groups print out, analyze, and revise columns.

19. Discuss the way a newspaper conveys its beliefs to the readers. (Explain that an editorial expresses the official stand of the paper as an institution.)
    A. What are the qualities of an editorial?
       1. Impersonal tone (editorial "we")
       2. Concern with issues—controversial, timely (often in same issue as the news story)
    B. Why are editorials important?
       1. Represent voice of the newspaper
       2. Seek to mold public opinion or spur action
       3. Keep opinions out of news columns

20. What is the form of an editorial?
    A. Thesis—one-or two-sentence introduction—which sets the tone and introduces the subject
    B. Logical progression of fact and opinion—issues cited and actions recommended
    C. Conclusion—firm statement

21. *Exercises:*
    A. Select several editorials from current newspapers. Groups analyze form and content.
    B. Ask what issue from fairy tale could be used for an editorial and discuss how to write it.

22. *Practice:* Students select news or school issue, gather facts, and write editorials. Groups print out, analyze, and revise editorials.

23. Discuss how students, as readers, can express their opinions to a newspaper.

24. *Exercise:* Students select issue, write, and revise letter to the editor, and mail it.

SUMMARY

Review reasons why newspapers are written in such standard and traditional form.

ADDITIONAL ACTIVITIES

1. *Literature:* Students select "news" item from class literature and write a news story, sidebar, and editorial on the issue or on a person involved.
2. *Vocabulary:* Students integrate vocabulary into their articles.
3. *Media:* Students watch TV news and listen to radio news to compare with newspaper reporting of same issue.

NOTES

Exercise for Item 8 (News items)

1. A gorilla escapes from the zoo.
2. A long-haired young man gives out flowers with a note attached on a subway station.
3. A bomb threat is made to the school.
4. A robot that can do homework is demonstrated.
5. A truck carrying radioactive wastes breaks down on a local street.

MODULE 14
MAGAZINES

AIM

To introduce students to magazine writing.

OBJECTIVES

By the end of this module, students will be able to

Write a utility article.
Write a personality sketch.

Write a personal experience article.

Write an interview.

Create individual mini-magazines.

MATERIALS

Magazines.

MOTIVATION

Students should be asked to bring in a magazine they are familiar with. Ask in class: What magazine did you select? What does it offer you?

PROCEDURE

1. Have students analyze their magazines, as follows:
   A. Read the table of contents and write what the list tells about the readers' interests.
   B. Look through the advertising and generalize about the average subscriber's income and living standards.
   C. What types of articles appear?
      1. fiction—to entertain, present ideas.
      2. news—to inform.
      3. features—to inform, guide, enlarge knowledge, entertain.
   D. Groups discuss their magazines.
2. Disucss the value of a utility or "how-to" article.
   A. Definition—helps people to help themselves
   B. Purpose—to help reader become healthier, wealthier, wiser, happier
3. Discuss some typical subjects of how-to articles (e.g., recipes, build-it-yourself, grow veggies on your windowsill, earn money in spare time).
4. Discuss quidelines for writers of a how-to piece:
   A. Is the idea a new one?
   B. Will it interest many readers?
   C. Is the idea practical?
5. *Exercises:*
   A. Have students analyze a how-to article in groups.
   B. Have groups select a fable (e.g., The Fox and the Grapes) and discuss what how-to articles could be derived from it.
6. *Practice:* Have students write a how-to piece on something they know. Groups print out, analyze, and revise copy.

7. Discuss the way magazines present information about people. Mention the characteristics of a personality sketch—that it includes details about the life of an important or famous person, shows achievements, describes how the subject overcame obstacles to acquire character, fame, or fortune.

8. Ask: How does the writer get information on the person?
   A. Printed sources—*Who's Who*, newspapers
   B. Interview with person
   C. Conversations with others who know him or her

9. Discuss what should be included in the article:
   A. Biographical data
   B. Description of person
   C. Quotes—about the subject's beliefs, advice, guidance to others
   D. Account of success
   E. Person's philosophy of life

10. *Exercises:*
    A. Each student selects a personality sketch from a magazine. Groups analyze the pieces.
    B. Students discuss a fable character as material for a personality sketch.

11. *Practice:* Students write a personality sketch about someone they know or a historical figure. Groups print out, analyze, and revise sketches.

12. Discuss how an interview article differs from a personality sketch.

13. Ask: What should you know before you interview the subject? (His or her background, interests, hobbies, likes, and dislikes.)

14. Discuss how to conduct an interview:
    A. Consider what the readers will want to know.
    B. Think of a list of questions.
    C. Take notes or tape record.

15. Talk about ways to put the information together into an article:
    A. Find an "angle" or "slant."
    B. Use material that proves the point.
    C. Discard anything irrelevant.

16. *Exercises:*
    A. Students analyze an interview article in groups.
    B. Students conduct a mock interview with a fable character and discuss how to write the article.
    C. Groups devise lists of questions they can use to interview someone they know.

17. *Practice:* Students use their lists of questions to interview someone (family member, store owner, businessman) and write the interview article. Groups print out, analyze, and revise the pieces.

18. Ask: How might something you have done become the focus of a magazine article? Personal experience provides interest, escape, ideas for similar situation.

19. Discuss possible topics (trip, work project, unusual accomplishment, solution to a problem.)
20. Consider ways to convince the readers of the authenticity and accuracy of the experience:
    A. Personal details
    B. Description of people, places, objects
    C. Conversations
21. *Exercises:*
    A. Groups read a personal-experience article and analyze. Then they brainstorm ideas that they could write about.
    B. Groups discuss how fable could be used for a personal-experience article.
22. *Practice:* Students write a personal-experience article. Groups print out, analyze, and revise articles.

SUMMARY

Review the types of writing that are likely to appear in a magazine.

SUMMARY ACTIVITY

Students print out articles of each type that they have written and compile and format collected articles as individual mini-magazines. They add a table of contents and other magazine features.

ADDITIONAL ACTIVITIES

1. *Literature:* Class literature can be used as focus for articles involving interview with character, personal experience of character, etc.
2. *Vocabulary:* Class vocabulary should be integrated into articles.
3. *Media:* Students study a particular magazine and slant an article toward it.

MODULE 15
RADIO

AIM

To consider the kind of writing done for radio broadcasts.

OBJECTIVES

By the end of this module, students will be able to

Write a news broadcast.

Produce an interview.

Prepare an outline for a talk show.

Schedule the writing for a music program.

MATERIALS

Disks with students' previous work.

MOTIVATION

Ask: Which radio station do you listen to? Why?

PROCEDURE

1. Consider the features radio stations provide:
   A. News
   B. Interviews
   C. Music
   D. Talk shows
   E. Live events (e.g., sports)
2. Ask whether news writing is the same for print and radio news. (Both involve gathering information, inverted pyramid, short sentences.)
3. Discuss ways in which the two kinds of news writing are different. (Fewer details, shorter sentences, direct sentences, delivery in radio news.)

4. *Exercise:* Students load a news article they have written previously and edit it for radio broadcast. Groups analyze results and revise.

5. *Practice:*
   A. Students take five issues from daily newspaper and rewrite for a mini-news broadcast. They can add a weather report, sports scores, and a commercial.
   B. Groups work on broadcasts to perfect timing and delivery.

6. Discuss the way interviews are done on radio. Discuss question techniques, use of tape recordings, editing.

7. *Exercise:* Have students work in groups to create questions for radio interview of the same person they interviewed for a magazine article. Have them discuss differences in techniques.

8. *Practice:* Students revise their original interviews and write the script for a short radio interview. Student groups meet to analyze and revise the scripts.

9. Some radio stations have "talk" shows. Ask how these work. (Expert speaks; host asks questions; callers ask questions.)

10. *Exercise:* Students work in groups to create format for a talk show on any topic (e.g., a famous inventor discussing his invention). They create the script for the guest, host, callers, and guest and host responses. Each group script is presented to the class.

11. Discuss: To what extent is music on the radio more than just music?

12. *Exercise:* Students select several songs they would play and write the disk jockey's script. Groups analyze and revise the selections and scripts.

SUMMARY

Review the way writing for radio differs from writing for any other medium.

ADDITIONAL ACTIVITIES

1. *Literature:* Students write scripts for interviews and talk shows using characters from class literature.

2. *Vocabulary:* Students integrate vocabulary into writing radio scripts. They can also invent a "vocabulary expert" for an interview or talk show.

3. *Media:* Students listen to examples of news, interviews, music, and talk-show broadcasts and analyze in terms of what they've learned.

MODULE 16
TELEVISION

AIM

To teach principles of TV scriptwriting.

OBJECTIVES

By the end of this module, students will be able to

> Create a script for a TV news broadcast.
> Write mini-scripts for a cartoon, a soap opera, and a situation comedy.
> Outline the format of a "special."
> Write a commercial.

MOTIVATION

Students should be asked in advance to itemize the program schedule for a television station for one day. (Use newspaper listings or TV Guide.)

PROCEDURE

1. Discuss the types of programs we find on television:
    A. News broadcasts and shows
    B. Cartoons
    C. Soap operas
    D. Situation comedies.
    E. Game shows
    F. Specials
2. Ask how television news is different from print and radio news coverage.
    A. How many items are covered in one broadcast?
    B. In what depth is each item examined?
    C. What type of story is the lead story?
    D. What difficulties are there in writing TV news?
3. *Exercise:* Have students work in groups to create an outline for the Six O'Clock News. Each student contributes the script for one or two segments. The group presents its broadcast to the class when all revisions are complete.

4. Ask what makes cartoons so popular.

5. Consider the typical story line for a cartoon.

6. *Exercise:* Students work in groups to create and revise the script for a TV mini-cartoon program. They should indicate the actions that would be on screen and use all of the elements of playwriting. Final scripts should be presented to the class.

7. Discuss the appeal of a soap opera.

8. Consider a typical soap opera story line.

9. *Exercise:* Students create a mini-soap opera episode using all of the elements of playwriting. Groups print out, analyze, and revise scripts. Final scripts should be presented to the class.

10. Discuss some examples of situation comedy.
    A. Why are they so popular?
    B. What categories do they fit into? (Police, hospital, etc.)

11. *Exercise:* Students create a mini-sitcom episode using all of the elements of playwriting. Groups analyze and revise the scripts. Final scripts should be presented to the class.

12. Ask what commercials are the most successful. Why?

13. *Exercise:* Students work in teams to write commercials. Small groups print out, analyze, and revise. The commercials should be presented to the class.

SUMMARY

Review the ways in which scriptwriting for TV is different from other scriptwriting.

ADDITIONAL ACTIVITIES

1. *Literature:* Students can select situations and/or characters from literature and rewrite an episode as a sitcom or soap opera.

2. *Vocabulary:* Students should integrate vocabulary into scripts.

3. *Media:* TV programs can be taped so they can be shown and analyzed in class. News broadcasts can be derived from soap opera events. Soap operas can also be created from real events in the news.

MODULE 17
LETTERS

AIM

To make students aware of the different kinds of correspondence that are possible.

OBJECTIVES

By the end of this module, students will be able to

Format and write friendly letters, invitations, directions, and thank you notes. Format and write business letters to request information, order materials, and complain to a company.

MOTIVATION

You are giving a party. Decide when and where it will be and what it will be for. Also select ten people you want to invite.

PROCEDURE

1. Have students write letters as invitations to this party. Discuss which type of letter form they should use. (The informal, friendly letter.)
2. Describe the parts of the friendly letter:
   A. Heading (return address and date)
   B. Salutation
   C. Body
   D. Closing
   E. Signature
3. *Exercise:*
   A. Students type friendly letter (invitation) on word processor and print out a copy. They discuss form and content in groups.
   B. Students use GLOBAL SEARCH and REPLACE to send the same invitation to a second friend.
4. *Exercise:* Tell students one of the friends they invited has never been to the place where the party will be held. Now they should write to this friend again to give directions.

    A. Discuss how to give clear directions.

    B. Enter text, print out copy.

    C. Students work in groups to revise.

5. Say: You had a terrific party. Best of all, your friends brought great gifts. Now you'll have to send thank-you notes.

    A. *Exercise:* Students use friendly letter form to write a thank-you note.

    B. Students work in groups to revise first letter so that most of it can be used for a second thank-you note.

6. Mention that some letters, called business letters, are intended to be sent to companies.

7. Discuss ways in which the business letter is different from the friendly letter:

    A. Form—includes inside address

    B. Content—short and to the point; formal style, not chatty

8. Ask for what purposes we would write to companies:

    A. To request information

    B. To order material

    C. To complain

9. Tell students they can't decide where they would like to go on vacation. What should they do? (Write letters to Chambers of Commerce requesting travel information.)

    Exercise:

    A. Create a letter that could be revised to send elsewhere.

    B. Groups print out, analyze, and revise ietters.

    C. Discuss results as a class.

10. Have students pretend they want to order a poster from a catalog. What should they do? (Write a letter that orders the specific poster and indicates the amount of money enclosed.)

    Exercise:

    A. Students create the letter.

    B. Groups print out and revise letters.

    C. Discuss results as a class.

11. Tell students they purchased an item (stereo, cereal, record, etc) and are not pleased with it. What should they do? (Write a letter stating the problem and what remedy is sought.

    Exercise:

    A. Students create the letter

    B. Groups print out and revise letter.

    C. Discuss results as a class.

SUMMARY

Review the purposes of writing letters.

ADDITIONAL ACTIVITIES

1. *Literature:*
   A. Write a friendly letter to a character from class literature.
   B. Write a business letter to the publisher requesting information.
2. *Vocabulary:* Students should integrate class vocabulary into their letters.
3. *Media:* Students can write to celebrities and companies in the news.

Section V
Writing for Exams

MODULE 18
LETTER OF COMPLAINT

Note: This topic was selected from the items in the New York State Regents Competency Test in Writing. It may apply to other minimum-competency examinations as well.

AIM

To teach students how to write a letter of complaint.

OBJECTIVES

By the end of this module, students will be able to

Use correct business-letter form.
Integrate the information given into the body of the letter.
Analyze the problem to find a solution.
Complete the letter with an acceptable solution.

MATERIALS

Motivation exercise, sample question, and another examination question should be stored on disk.

MOTIVATION

    A. Load exercise from disk. Students read to decide which arguments are convincing and why.

    B. Have students pretend they bought snacks which tasted terrible. If the store won't take them back, what can the students do? (Write a letter of complaint to the company.) What should the letter say?

PROCEDURE

1. Discuss the purpose of a business letter of complaint.

2. Load sample question from disk. Students read question and discuss the situation.

3. Say: If we wish to use what is on the screen so we avoid retyping anything, what must we do? (Have students perform tasks after naming them.)
       A. Insert heading, inside address, and salutation.
       B. Check for correct spelling and punctuation.

4. Ask what changes we have to make in the question before using the given words in our letters.
       A. Change person from "you" to "I."
          (We can use GLOBAL SEARCH and REPLACE.)
       B. Delete address information.

5. Say: If this situation really happened to us, and we were writing to complain, what should we tell the company next? (What we want done about the problem.)

6. Ask for some possible solutions.

7. Have students enter a second paragraph in which they tell the company what they want done. Groups evaluate and revise second paragraphs.

8. The letter is almost finished. What is needed to complete it? (Closing and signature.) Students perform the final task.

9. *Practice:* Load another examination question from disk. Students use this question and repeat the procedure they just learned to practice answering the question individually. Groups evaluate results and revise letters.

SUMMARY

Review the steps we follow to answer this type of examination question.

NOTES

Exercise for Motivation

You enjoy eating pretzels as a snack, but you see an advertisement for "Nutrient Snaks." Which reasons would convince you to try the new snack?

1. Baseball star Darryl Strawberry eats Nutrient Snaks every day.
2. The great taste is what Californians are talking about.
3. Nutrient Snaks are made from a special formula by elves.
4. Nutrient Snaks are made in an electronically controlled factory.
5. The name alone tells you you're missing something if you don't eat Nutrient Snaks.
6. Try it or you'll never know what you're missing.

Exercise for Item 2 (Sample question)

After your vacation, you sent a roll of film to be developed to Class Color Photo and enclosed a check for $3.95. When you received the pictures, they were all blurred and smudged. You must write to the company at Post Office Box 21, Madison, Wisconsin 34567.

MODULE 19
FROM OUTLINE TO ESSAY

AIM

To help students write logical, organized essays.

OBJECTIVES

By the end of this module, students will be able to

> Create paragraphs in a structured form.
> Use the Harvard outline to organize thoughts.
> Write a structured essay.

MATERIALS

Motivation exercise and empty Harvard outlines should be stored on disk. See Notes. Sample outline and composition for exercise are also in the Notes.

MOTIVATION

Load the exercise involving Jenny's list of excuses from disk. Students read and decide which items on the list were important. They then discuss their answers and consider why Jenny should have given only pertinent reasons.

PROCEDURE

1. Ask students to name the reasons why people take up physical exercise.
2. Say: If we wanted to write a composition (essay) about why exercise is good for people, how would we begin?
    A. Jot down ideas.
    B. Consider what evidence proves those ideas.
3. Review: Let's begin with a paragraph. What is the first element?
    A. Topic Sentence
    B. Elicit topic sentence for paragraph about exercise.

4. What element is next?
   A. Proof—two or more sentences giving reasons, explanations, or details
   B. Elicit two proof sentences for paragraph about exercise.

5. What is the last element in a paragraph?
   A. Clincher—sentence that sums up ideas and leads to next paragraph
   B. Elicit clincher sentence for paragraph about exercise.

6. Since it is difficult to brainstorm ideas and write them in an organized way as we are thinking, what steps should we follow to produce the best ideas we can and the best writing we can do?
   A. Write notes.
   B. Organize the notes.
   C. Write.
   D. Revise.

7. One method for organizing notes is called outlining.
   A. Load empty Harvard outline (modified form) from disk.
   B. *Exercise:* Have students use ideas from paragraph about exercise to fill in Section I of Harvard outline. Discuss results.

8. Now have students jot down notes, ideas for the rest of the composition.
   A. Students write notes.
   B. Teacher demonstrates that the ideas for the rest of the composition have been posed in the introductory paragraph.
   Note: The structure of a composition is like the structure of an individual paragraph.
   1. Introductory paragraph introduces ideas that will be covered.
   2. Two or three paragraphs expand ideas by giving proof.
   3. Concluding paragraph sums up and ties composition together.
   C. Work with students to create outline for second and third paragraphs (proof paragraphs). The ideas come from their notes.

9. Take Section II of outline and work with class to create second paragraph of composition. Discuss logic of this type of structure.

10. Take Section III of outline and work with class to create third paragraph of composition.

11. Discuss what goes into a concluding paragraph. (Summary reinforces point that was made and establishes completion.)

12. Work with students to complete the outline (Section IV) and to create a conclusion for the composition about exercise.

13. Most compositions are more sophisticated than this one about exercise, but the technique is always the same.
    A. Load expanded form of Harvard outline from disk.
    B. Discuss how we fill in the blanks.

14. *Exercise:*
    A. Students select their own topics and create outline (modified form) for whichever topic they have chosen.

B.   Small groups analyze and revise outlines.
C.   Students use outlines to create compositions.
D.   Small groups meet to analyze and revise compositions.

SUMMARY

Review techniques that promote logical, organized writing.

NOTES

Exercise for Motivation

Jenny is a student in this school. Yesterday she was an hour late. When her teacher asked her why, she said the following five things:
1.   My sister called from college just as I was leaving.
2.   My newspaper was late.
3.   I overslept; I must not have set the alarm.
4.   The bus broke down.
5.   I tried to call you (the teacher) at home, but you had left already.

HARVARD OUTLINE (modified form)

I
    A.
    B.
II
    A.
    B.
III
    A.
    B.
IV
    A.
    B.

HARVARD OUTLINE (expanded form)

I
    A.
        1.
        2.

       B.
           1.
           2
 II
       A.
           1.
           2.
       B.
           1.
           2.
 III
       A.
           1.
           2.
       B.
           1.
           2.
 IV
       A.
           1.
           2.
       B.
           1.
           2.

**SAMPLE OUTLINE AND COMPOSITION
ON EXERCISE**

 I   Exercise is good
       A. Body
       B. Mind
 II Body
       A. Muscle Tone
       B. Weight Control
 III Mind
       A. Thinking Ability
       B. Wakefulness
 IV Exercise helps
       A. Body
       B. Mind

    Exercise is beneficial for every human being. A person's body is helped by a
program of daily activity. Also, a person will find that his intellectual capacity is

increased if he exercises consistently. Without a doubt, exercise is one of the greatest boons to mankind.

First of all, a human's body will have renewed strength and stamina if he follows a regimen of even minor exercise daily. Every muscle that is exercised will grow firmer and stronger; thus, muscle tone is improved. In addition, exercising regularly is a proved method of weight control; burning calories in physical activity leads to a slender body. Thus, you see how your body will benefit from exercise.

Second, a person's mind will benefit from physical exercise as well. Exercise releases hormones which stimulate the brain into activity and promote a sense of well being. Thus a person who exercises will be able to think well. Furthermore, the increased energy that is derived from daily exercise will affect a person's ability to prolong mental activity; sleepiness can be fought off with exercise. Therefore, you can see that your brain will be spurred into activity if you exercise.

It should be evident that there is much to gain from a regular program of physical exercise. Your body will grow stronger and slimmer. Your mind will be capable of renewed vigor. Thus, we see the reasons why daily exercise improves the quality of life of those who follow "the doctor's orders."

MODULE 20
COMPOSITION OF PERSUASION

Note: This topic was selected from the items in the New York State Regents Competency Test in Writing. It may apply to other minimum-competency examinations, college-placement tests, and other persuasive-essay writing assignments.

AIM

To explore techniques that can help make a written argument persuasive.

OBJECTIVES

By the end of this module, students will be able to

Use a logical progression of detail to convince.
Use the Harvard outline and correct paragraph and composition forms.
Write a composition of persuasion.

MATERIALS

Persuasive-essay question in Notes and another examination question should be stored on disk.

MOTIVATION

Say: Suppose you wanted to go to another state with your science club this summer. How would you convince your parents to let you go?

PROCEDURE

1. Remind students that in any essay or argument, they must be aware of the following:
   A. What the issue is
   B. Who the audience is: whom they are trying to convince
   C. What their purpose is
   D. What arguments will achieve the effect they want
2. Ask students what arguments work best when they want to convince someone to do something or to permit them to do something.
   A. Point out benefits to the person hearing the argument.
   B. Point out benefit to the person making the argument.
   C. Point out benefits to society.
3. Have students write the notes they might use for a letter to their parents seeking permission to go away.
   A. Elicit issue.
   B. Elicit audience.
   C. Elicit purpose.
   D. Elicit arguments. (Keep in mind the points in Item 2.)
4. Point out that once we have the notes, our next step is to organize these into a logical progression of ideas and put them into the Harvard outline.
5. Groups organize the ideas into outline form.
6. Ask students how we would use the outline to write the letter (composition). Review procedure used in Module 19.
7. Now have class look at a different issue, persuading someone to adopt a certain point of view. Load sample question from disk.
8. *Exercise:* Elicit the questions and have students write answers to them. Class discusses each as it is completed.
   A. What do we ask ourselves first?
      1. What is the issue?
      2. Write the issue.

B. What do we ask next?
    1. Who is the audience?
    2. Write who the audience is.
C. What do we decide next?
    1. What is our purpose?
    2. Write the purpose.
D. What is the last step in note writing?
    1. What arguments will work?
    2. Write the arguments.

9. Have students organize their notes into outline form. Groups analyze and revise outlines.

10. Have students use outlines to write compositions. Groups analyze and revise compositions.

11. *Practice:* Load an actual question from disk. Students answer the question by repeating the procedure above individually. After all work is completed, groups evaluate and revise.

SUMMARY

Review steps we use to guarantee success with a compositon of persuasion.

NOTES

Sample persuasion question

The mayor of your town has asked for student opinion about placing shelters for homeless people in stable residential areas of your community. Decide if you agree or disagree with the plan. Write a composition of about 200 words stating your opinion to the mayor. Give two reasons for your opinion. Explain each reason.

MODULE 21
GENERAL COMPOSITION TOPICS

Note: This topic was selected from the items in the New York State Comprehensive Examination in English. It is applicable to other formal examinations, college-placement tests, and other writing assignments.

AIM

To help students write compositions in situations that require logical organization.

OBJECTIVES

By the end of this module, students will be able to

Select a topic carefully.
Organize their thoughts.
Write an effective composition.

MATERIALS

Motivation exercise (question only), sample composition topics, and other examination topics should be stored on disk. See Notes.

MOTIVATION

A. Load exercise from disk. Have students solve and discuss answers.
B. Ask how students got the right answers. (By sorting information.)
C. Ask how the sorting technique applies to writing compositions.

PROCEDURE

1. Ask why composition questions are so important on examinations.
2. Load sample topics from disk. Discuss how we pick the topic we want.
    A. Divide topics into two categories:
        1. General—within our own experience

> 2. Specific—requiring specific information
B. Students categorize list in front of them and write the issue for each.
C. Discuss what information would be necessary in order to write on specific topics.

3. Discuss which topic each student would select and the reasons for that selection.

4. Discuss methods we could use to develop any of the topics:
   A. Advantages and disadvantages
   B. Comparison and contrast
   C. Cause and effect
   D. Examples
   E. Chronological order

5. Discuss how to handle each topic using the methods listed in Item 4.

6. *Exercise:* Students select one topic each and follow the procedure for note writing for essays.
   A. What is the issue?
   B. Who is the audience?
   C. What is your purpose?
   D. What method will you use?
   E. What details support your purpose?

7. Groups analyze and revise notes.

8. Students create an outline from their notes and meet in small groups to evaluate and revise outlines.

9. Students write compositions. Groups evaluate and revise compositions.

10. *Practice:* Students select another topic and follow the procedure to create a composition individually. Groups evaluate and revise after composition has been written.

11. *Practice:* Other composition topics can be used for additional practice.

SUMMARY

Review steps in writing a good composition.

NOTES

Exercise for Motivation

Three students, Tony, Rosie, and Debbie, decided to clean up their classroom. One washed the chalkboard; one sorted all the books, and one picked up papers. Tony did not wash the chalkboard. Rosie did not pick up papers. Debbie did not pick up papers or sort books. Who did what?

Answers: Tony picked up papers.

Rosie sorted books.

Debbie washed the chalkboard.

Sample composition topics

Directions: Write a well-organized composition of 250-300 words on one of the following topics:

The Future

Promises

Medical Treatment for Senior Citizens

Illegal Aliens

The Quality of Television Programs

When A Fantasy Comes True

Equal Rights for Women

Success

The Cabbage Patch Phenomenon

Welfare Reform

Funds for Education

MODULE 22
LITERATURE ESSAY

Note: This topic was selected from the items in the New York State Comprehensive Examination in English. It may be used for book-report writing as well.

AIM

To give students practice answering a literature question.

OBJECTIVES

By the end of this module, students will be able to

Analyze a literature question.

Generalize clearly.

Show familiarity with the works of literature they are discussing.

Use specific references.

Write a literature essay.

MATERIALS

Exercise for Motivation and sample literature questions should be stored on disk. See Notes.

MOTIVATION

A. Ask: What is a literature essay? (Demonstration of knowledge about works of literature and ability to organize this knowledge into logical form for a specific purpose.)

B. Load exercise from disk. Students decide which items are true.

C. Ask students what this exercise has to do with literature essays. (It involves making inferences, using only information that is correct and appropriate.)

PROCEDURE

1. Load sample questions from disk.
2. Ask how we pick which essay we will do.
   A. Read the questions.
   B. Decide for which question we can come up with the most appropriate works of literature.
3. Ask how we can analyze the questions.
   A. What is the issue?
   B. What is my purpose? (Note: Discuss how literature question often asks us to write about values and social and moral issues.)
   C. What types of literature are relevant to the question?
   D. What works of literature are appropriate?
   E. What specific references can we use for each?
4. Review types of literature and elicit examples.
   A. Novel
   B. Full-length play
   C. Biography
   D. Book of true experience
   E. Short story
   F. One-act play

G. Essay

H. Poem

5. Use question A and have students analyze the question and write notes. (Note: Stress that definite references mean references to specific incidents, characters, or ideas, not plot summaries.) Groups discuss and revise notes.

6. Ask how we should organize these notes. (Harvard outline)

7. Students organize notes into outline form. (Note: They must provide for introduction and conclusion as in any other essay.) Groups analyze and revise outlines.

8. Students use outlines to write literature essay. Groups evaluate and revise essays.

9. Use question B and have students repeat the procedure individually to produce notes and outlines. Groups analyze and revise after outlines are completed.

10. Students write essays from outlines. Groups evaluate and revise essays.

11. *Practice:* Actual literature questions can be used for additional practice.

SUMMARY

Review purpose of the literature essay.

NOTES

Exercise for Motivation

Jack and Jill went up the hill
To fetch a pail of water.
Jack fell down
And broke his crown.
And Jill came tumbling after.

1. Jack was angry at Jill.

2. Jack and Jill ran up the hill.

3. They carried a pail up the hill.

4. The water spilled.

5. People who run up hills fall down.

6. They fell down because they went up.

7. They were the only two people to go up that hill.

8. Jill was fat.

9. Jack fell first.
10. Jill started to cry.

Sample literature questions

Directions: Write a well-organized composition of 200-250 words on A or B.

A. Making an important decision can be an occasion for personal growth or an instance of defeat. From the plays, novels, biographies, and books of true experience you have read, choose two. For each, choose one character who had to make an important decision. Describe the situation for each, and tell how it was an occasion for growth or for defeat. In each case, show the effect making the decision has on his or her life. Give titles and authors.

B. As part of your community's renewed interest in reading improvement, your parent-teacher association has arranged for some students to visit English classes for brief presentations encouraging other students to read. You have been asked to prepare four separate presentations that will highlight specific short works. Your directions are to select four works from the short stories, one-act plays, essays, and poems you have read (in any combination) and write the presentation for each that will inspire other students to read the work. Include the title, author, and at least one specific reason why a person should read the work. Your reasons should reflect your knowledge of the works.

MODULE 23
REPORTS FROM NOTES

Note: This topic was selected from the items in the New York State Regents Competency Test in Writing. It may apply to other report-writing assignments.

AIM

To teach students how to use notes to create a report.

OBJECTIVES

By the end of this module, students will be able to

Discern the topic of the report.

Categorize items and label categories.

Arrange notes in order.

Write the report.

MATERIALS

Motivation exercise, sample question in Notes, and another report question should be stored on disk.

MOTIVATION

A. Load exercise from disk. Students figure out who is who.

B. Ask: How did we figure out the answers? (Sort information into categories.)

PROCEDURE

1. Ask how this technique applies to a report question.
2. Load sample question from disk. Have students read the question and notes.
3. Ask what the issue (topic) is.
4. Ask who the audience is.
5. Ask what students' purpose is.
6. Procedure for notes. Students perform each task and discuss and revise results in groups.
    A. Sort the notes into groups (categories) using BLOCK MOVES. (Find similarities among items.)
    B. Label each category. (Label can be an item in the notes or their own.) These categories will become items as in an outline. (Imposing outline form is optional.)
    C. Arrange the notes in each category in order. (Use BLOCK MOVES.)
7. Procedure for writing: Students perform each task and discuss and revise results in groups.
    A. Create an introduction from the question and general information in the notes.
    B. Expand note phrases into sentences.
    C. Align sentences to form paragraphs.
    D. Add a conclusion.
    E. Add transitional words or phrases and other sentences as needed.
8. Check for paragraph completion. Revise and proofread.
9. Groups evaluate and revise completed reports.

10. *Practice:* Load another report question from disk. Have students answer the question by repeating the procedure above individually. After all work is completed, groups evaluate and revise.

SUMMARY

Review steps we use to guarantee success with a report question.

NOTES

Exercise for Motivation

A spider, a chimpanzee, a zebra, and an elephant live in the zoo together. Their names are Ella, Charlie, Susie, and Zeke. Which name belongs to which animal?

1. Susie is older than the elephant.
2. Both Charlie and the chimpanzee are larger than Zeke.
3. The chimpanzee likes Ella, who is the oldest.

Answers: Ella Zebra
 Charlie Elephant
 Susie Chimpanzee
 Zeke Spider

Sample report question

Directions: Write a report using the situation and the set of notes given below. Read all the information before you start to write.

You visited a television studio and learned how a variety show is produced. You are reporting what you learned to your English class. The notes you took are as follows:

Writers plan out what will be in the show
During broadcast, director sits in control room to tell cameras where to move
Singers and dancers rehearse
Star memorizes his lines
Star comes out and begins show with a funny speech
Cameramen and director decide where cameras will be for each shot
Live audience applauds when applause sign lights up
Performers do their very best since this is the real thing

At dress rehearsal, everyone goes through all steps of actual show

Show actually stops while commercials, which are on tape, are broadcast over the air.

Organize these notes into a written report. Be sure to include all the information in the notes.

Section VI
Scholarly Writing

MODULE 24
REPORTS AND TERM PAPERS

AIM

To teach students how to prepare reports and term papers.

OBJECTIVES

By the end of this module, students will be able to

> Select a subject.
> Decide on a topic (issue).
> State the objective.
> Locate sources of information.
> Prepare an outline.
> Take notes.
> Write a report.
> Prepare a bibliography.

MATERIALS

Question for Motivation should be on disk. See Notes.

MOTIVATION

Load exercise from disk.

A. Students answer the questions.
B. How do we get answers to questions like these? (Own knowledge, observation, research, interview.)

NOTE: This module should be correlated with visits to the library. Subjects should be assigned so that students can follow the procedure as outlined below. Groups monitor progress after each step.

PROCEDURE

1. Ask students where to look for information when writing a report.
2. Discuss procedure for deciding what subject to write about:
    A. Determine what own interest is.
    B. Understand the limits of the assignment.
    C. Understand the limits of resources.
3. Ask how we narrow the subject into a topic (issue).
    A. Read background article in encyclopedia.
    B. Ask questions: Who?, What?, Where?, When?, Why?, How?
4. Ask students to state their purpose:
    A. Determine the point they want to make.
    B. Write a statement of purpose (a sentence telling what they are trying to prove, demonstrate, or describe). This should present an angle or argument that can be supported with research (not an indisputable fact or a personal opinion that can't be supported with research).
5. Ask students where to get information (own knowledge, observation, interview, research).
6. Discuss how to look things up:
    A. Card catalog (fiction, non-fiction, biography)
        Types of cards: title, author, subject
    B. *Reader's Guide to Periodical Literature*
    C. *New York Times Index*
    D. Reference section (*Who's Who, Facts on File*, etc.)

7. Ask: How do we know what to look up?
   A. Refer to statement of purpose.
   B. Divide statement into categories for investigation (Who?, What?, Where?, etc.).
   C. Prepare an outline from categories.

8. Discuss what to do with the books and articles we find:
   A. Prepare a working bibliography—list of sources (title, author, date and city of publication, publisher, page number).
   B. Take notes:
      1. Summary of what was said
      2. Direct quotes
   C. Use note cards:
      1. Fill out a separate card for each idea.
      2. Indicate category from outline.
      3. Write title and page number.
   D. Footnotes and bibliography.

9. Discuss what to do when notes are complete:
   A. Sort note cards into categories.
   B. Modify outline based on information located:
      1. Delete items not found.
      2. Insert items and details found.
   C. Write report from outline. Note: Procedure from Module 23 should be used to write report.
   D. Prepare footnotes.
   E. Prepare bibliography.
   F. Revise report.

10. If you have access to a file-management program and on-line information services, students can create their reports completely electronically. A system of note-keeping on the word processor can be demonstrated and utilized, or students can use the word processor solely for the report-writing portion of this module.

SUMMARY

Review the steps we use in preparing and writing reports and term papers.

NOTES

Exercise for Motivation

1. How old are you?
2. How many windows are in this room?
3. When was the Empire State building constructed?
4. When did you get your first tooth?

Section VII

Grammar and Usage

MODULE 25
PARTS OF SPEECH

AIMS

To review the principal parts of speech and our use of them.

OBJECTIVES

By the end of this module, students will be able to

> Define the parts of speech.
> Identify the parts of speech.
> Use the parts of speech.

MATERIALS

Exercise stored on disk. See Notes.

MOTIVATION

Ask: How do we play Mad Libs?

PROCEDURE

1. What does the phrase "parts of speech" mean? (The identification of words according to their use in a sentence.)
2. There are eight principal parts of speech. Let's identify, define, and give an example for each. (Elicit responses from the class.)
   A. Noun
   B. Pronoun
   C. Adjective
   D. Verb
   E. Adverb
   F. Preposition
   G. Conjunction
   H. Interjection
3. *Exercise:* Construct a sentence using the word processor.
   A. Type a noun.
   B. Type a verb.
   C. Insert an adjective.
   D. Insert an adverb.
   E. Add a preposition (and its phrase).
   F. Add a conjunction and another noun.
   G. Insert an interjection.
   H. Add a capital letter to start the sentence, a period to end it, and change anything that may not have worked out quite right.
4. *Exercise:* Silly sayings (using the word processor).
   A. Create a list of nouns and adjectives that start with the same letters (Silly Sally, dreadful Doberman).
   B. Create a list of verbs and adverbs that start with the same letters (climbs clumsily, eats eagerly).
   C. Use BLOCK MOVES to join noun/adjective with verb/adverb.
   D. Insert modifiers to create silly sentences.
   E. Discuss results and revise in groups.
5. Mad Libs
   A. Use Mad Libs from disk.
   B. Students create Mad Libs.
      1. Create a Mad Libs screen: Type passage and put part of speech to be inserted in parentheses.
      2. Ask another student to list his answers to the parts of speech you request.
      3. Fill in the blanks.
      4. Show other students your combined effort.
   Note: This activity can be used by the whole group as well.

SUMMARY

Review purposes the parts of speech serve.

Activity

Have students load a passage from their own file disks and check for correct use of the parts of speech.

ADDITIONAL ACTIVITIES

1. *Literature:* Use a passage from the literature the class is studying. Store on disk with words omitted. Leave spaces and indicate part of speech of missing words. Have students insert from a list or from memory.
2. *Vocabulary:* Store list of class vocabulary on disk. Below the list, type sentences with words omitted and parts of speech indicated. Have students insert correct word into each.
3. *Advanced vocabulary:* Same as Item 2 but students must change part of speech of listed words.
4. *Media:* Store headlines from daily newspaper on disk. Students indicate part of speech of each word. Then they write their own headlines using parts of speech in the same manner.

NOTES

Mad Libs Exercise

(Plural noun) were heard in the corridor outside the (noun). Angela said, "I am (adjective)," The (adjective) boy near her said (adverb), "It's only a (adjective) (noun) that you hear."

"I want to see (pronoun)," (verb) (proper noun). They raced (preposition) the (noun) and looked.

"Oh, no," said Angela.

"Oh, no," (verb) another girl.

It was a (noun).

MODULE 26
PARTS OF A SENTENCE

AIMS

To review the parts of a sentence and our use of them.

OBJECTIVES

By the end of this module, students will be able to

Define, identify, and use subjects.
Define, identify, and use predicates.
Define, identify, and use phrases.

MATERIALS

Exercises stored on disk. See Notes.

MOTIVATION

Assign students parts of speech. Then have each student say a word aloud to create a sentence. Other students may add to complete the sentence (e.g., "Starving Sylvester ate noisily in school.").

PROCEDURE

1. Ask: How did we combine all of these parts of speech to create a sentence that others can understand?
2. Ask class to define a sentence.
3. Discuss what parts of the sentence are needed to make a sentence whole. (Use motivation sentence to illustrate. Add to it to demonstrate parts not included.) Elicit responses from class.
   A. Subject
   B. Predicate
   C. Phrase

    D. Object

    E. Complement

4. *Exercise:* Matching

    A. Load file with lists of subjects and predicates.

    B. Use BLOCK MOVES to create combinations. Insert capitals, adjectives, etc., to make sentences complete.

    C. Insert objects or complements into each.

    D. Have students discuss and revise results with a partner.

5. *Exercise:* Add a part (one at a time).

    A. Type a subject, verb, indirect object, direct object (e.g., "We gave the gorilla bananas.").

    B. Type a subject, verb, complement (e.g., "He ate them neatly.").

    C. Insert a phrase into each sentence.

6. *Exercise:* The uses of phrases

    A. Type a sentence.

    B. Add a phrase that tells something about a noun in your sentence (adjectival phrase).

    C. Add a phrase that tells something about a verb or adjective in your sentence (adverbial phrase).

    D. Discuss and revise results with a partner.

7. *Exercise:* Story line

    A. Load mini-story from disk. Identify parts of each sentence.

    B. Create your own story line as in the example.

SUMMARY

Review the function each part of a sentence serves.

Activity

Have students load a passage from their own file disks and check for correct use of the parts of their sentences.

ADDITIONAL ACTIVITIES

1. *Literature:* Create a story line to summarize the plot of the literature that the class is studying. Identify parts of each sentence.

2. *Vocabulary:* Use class vocabulary list to create silly sentences. Begin by creating subjects and predicates as in Item 4 above.

3. *Media:* Students analyze television listings from the newspaper. Then they write their own TV listing.

NOTES

Exercise for Item 4 (Subjects and predicates)

SUBJECTS	PREDICATES
the rotten apple	smiled foolishly
a tired chimpanzee	rolled away
a sleepy student	jumped crazily

Exercise for Item 7 (Story line)

1. Agatha was a tiny goldfish.
2. Tom Cat was hungry.
3. Tom ate Agatha.
4. Agatha squirmed in Tom's stomach.
5. Agatha was digested.
6. Tom felt sick.

MODULE 27
CLAUSES AND SENTENCE TYPES

AIMS

To introduce clauses and how are they used, and to explain how different kinds of clauses produce different types of sentences.

OBJECTIVES

By the end of this module, students will be able to

Define, identify, and use independent and dependent clauses.
Create sentences of four types: simple, compound, complex, and compound-complex.

MATERIALS

Exercise stored on disk. See Notes.

MOTIVATION

Load clause from disk, and ask students how we can make this into a sentence.

PROCEDURE

1. Ask what are the two parts of our completed sentence. (Elicit definitions of independent clause, dependent clause.)
2. Ask how a clause can be used:
    A. As an adjective—"That is a dog who chases pigeons."
    B. As a noun—I wonder who chases pigeons in the park?
    C. As an adverb—"He stays wherever he can chase pigeons."
3. Ask how adjective and noun clauses are inserted into sentences. (Via connecting words: *who, that*.)
4. Ask how adverbial clauses are inserted. (Via subordinating conjunctions: *after, if, since, while, until*.)
5. *Exercise:* Adding clauses
    A. Look at sentence 1 from disk.
    B. Insert a clause that acts as an adjective (e.g., "who sings in the shower").
    C. Insert a clause that acts as an adverb (e.g., "while she scrubbed).
    D. Add a clause that acts as a noun (e.g., "whoever would listen").
    E. Create your own sentence with all of these elements.
    F. Discuss and revise sentences with a partner.
6. *Exercise:* Types of Sentences
    A. Look at sentences 2 and 3 from disk.
    B. Ask what this type of sentence is called (a simple sentence).
    C. Use edit functions to join these two sentences (e.g., "The gorilla is here, and he wants a banana.")
    D. Ask what this type of sentence is called (a compound sentence).
    E. Insert a word that makes one part of the sentence a dependent clause (e.g., "When the gorilla is here, he wants a banana.")
    F. Ask what this type of sentence is called (a complex sentence).
    G. Add another independent clause (e.g., "When the gorilla is, here he wants a banana, and then he goes home.")
    H. Ask what this type of sentence is called (a compound-complex sentence).
    I. Create simple sentences of your own and repeat the procedure.
    J. Create simple sentences and let another student repeat the procedure. Discuss results together.

SUMMARY

Review the purposes of different types of clauses.

Activity

Have students load a passage from their own file disks and check for correct use of clauses and sentence types.

ADDITIONAL ACTIVITIES

1. *Literature:* Store a passage from the literature the class is reading. Have students analyze for types of sentences the author used. They may edit the sentences to alter the type.
2. *Vocabulary:* Store class vocabulary list. Students use the words to create sentences of different types.
3. *Media:*
   A. Students analyze a newspaper article for sentence types.
   B. Students create sentences of various types from newspaper headlines.

NOTES

Motivation exercise (Clause)

who chases pigeons

Sentences for Items 5 and 6:

1. Goldy Fish gave a concert.
2. The gorilla is here.
3. He wants a banana.

MODULE 28
AGREEMENT

AIMS

To review agreement between subjects and verbs and between pronouns and their antecedents.

OBJECTIVES

By the end of this module, students will be able to

Explain how subjects and verbs agree in number.
Use subjects and verbs that agree in number.
Explain how antecedents and pronouns agree in number and gender.
Use antecedents and pronouns that agree in number and gender.

MATERIALS

Exercise stored on disk. See Notes.

MOTIVATION

Play the game called "How many animals?".
Load list of words from disk. Have students write one sentence for each word that shows how many of each animal are present. Discuss results.

PROCEDURE

1. Discuss regular spelling rules for changing singular words into plurals
2. *Exercise:* (Load from disk.) Say: We have a group of students who are singing. Let's use the present tense and fill in the correct verb to go with each noun or pronoun. Discuss results.
3. The verb of a sentence should agree with the subject in number. To check

themselves, students can look for the letter "s." Singular nouns do not have an "s"; singular verbs do. Plural nouns end in "s"; plural verbs don't.

4. *Exercise:* Trick sentences. Students must use the correct form of the verb in spite of
   A. phrases between subject and verb
   B. indefinite pronouns used as subjects
   C. collective nouns
   Students discuss and revise results with a partner.

5. Students create their own sentences to form a story line. They must use the tricks in Item 4. They discuss and revise sentences with a partner.

6. *Exercise:* Compound subjects
   Load examples from disk. Students insert correct form of the verbs.

7. Students create their own silly story line using compound subjects. Students discuss and revise story lines in groups.

8. Exercise: Agreement of pronoun and antecedent.
   Load examples from disk. Students fill in blanks and discuss and revise results with a partner.

9. Students create own story line using pronoun/antecedent agreement correctly. Groups discuss and revise story line.

SUMMARY

Review the reasons for observing agreement in writing.

Activity

Have students load a passage from their own file disks and check for correct use of agreement.

ADDITIONAL ACTIVITIES

1. *Literature:* Students write a plot summary of class literature using sentences that contain agreement.

2. *Vocabulary:* Load vocabulary list onto disk. Students create sentences that contain agreement for these words.

3. *Media:*
   A. Students find headlines and rewrite sentences using agreement.
   B. Students create summary of TV show using sentences with agreement.

NOTES

Motivation game: How many animals?

fish   moose   sheep   deer

Exercise for Item 2 (Use correct forms of the verb "sing.")

1. The boy _ _ _ _ _ _.
2. She _ _ _ _ _ _.
3. One student _ _ _ _ _ _.
4. They _ _ _ _ _ _.
5. We _ _ _ _ _ _.
6. Many students _ _ _ _ _ _.

Exercise for Item 4 (Trick sentences)

1. The baggy pants of the clown _ _ _ _ _ _ silly.
2. I see that every one of the ants _ _ _ _ _ _ across my picnic blanket.
3. Both of the gorillas _ _ _ _ _ _ happy today.
4. Most of that book _ _ _ _ _ _ interesting to read.
5. Most of the zebra's stripes _ _ _ _ _ _ painted evenly.
6. This class _ _ _ _ _ _ the smartest.
7. A herd of elephants _ _ _ _ _ _ heading this way.

Exercise for Item 6

1. Harry Hyena and Matilda Mermaid _ _ _ _ _ _ swimming together today.
2. Harry Hyena or Matilda Mermaid _ _ _ _ _ _ swimming too close to Alvin Alligator.
3. Alvin and the two friends _ _ _ _ _ _ going to argue.
4. Alvin or the two friends _ _ _ _ _ _ going to win the argument.

Exercise for Item 8

1. Alvin Alligator did _ _ _ _ _ _ best to steal Matilda away from Harry.
2. Matilda talked to Alvin for a while, but then _ _ _ _ _ _ decided that _ _ _ _ _ _ likes Harry better.
3. Neither Harry nor Alvin opened _ _ _ _ _ _ mouth to talk to each other.
4. Harry and Matilda swam away with _ _ _ _ _ _ noses high in the air.

MODULE 29
PUNCTUATION

AIMS

To demonstrate why we need punctuation and how to punctuate correctly.

OBJECTIVES

By the end of this module, students will be able to

Explain the uses of various types of punctuation.
Use end marks, commas, semicolons, apostrophes, and quotation marks correctly in their writing.

MATERIALS

Exercises stored on disk. See Notes.

MOTIVATION

Punctuate the following sentence three ways:
There are goons in this class.

PROCEDURE

1. Discuss the uses of the three different end marks:
   A. Period
   B. Question Mark
   C. Exclamation point
2. *Exercise:* Load sentences from disk. Have students use different end marks to punctuate. Discuss results and revise with a partner.
3. *Practice:* Students create a brief story as in the exercise above and punctuate as above. Discuss results and revise with a partner.
4. Commas: Load exercise from disk. Discuss uses for commas and insert them where needed:

   A. To separate items in a series

   B. To separate two or more adjectives before a noun

   C. To separate independent clauses (before a conjunction)

   D. To separate nonessential information from the rest of the sentence

   E. To set off introductory items

   F. To set off items that interrupt the sentence

5. *Practice:* Students create story line as in Item 4. Their sentences must demonstrate the uses of commas. Discuss results with a partner.

6. Discuss when we use semicolons (to separate independent clauses in compound sentences).

7. *Exercise:* Replace the commas and conjunctions in the sentences stored on disk with semi-colons. Discuss results with a partner.

8. *Practice:* Students create their own compound sentences with semicolons. Discuss and revise results with a partner.

9. *Exercise:* What belongs to whom?
   Load examples from disk. Students edit sentences using apostrophes and discuss the uses for apostrophes:
   A. Possession
   B. To indicate a letter has been omitted.

10. *Practice:* Students create their own lists of sentences with apostrophes. Discuss lists and revise with a partner.

11. Ask: How do we show the words that someone actually said when we write?

12. *Exercise:* Who said what? (Quotation marks)
    Students should insert quotation marks and punctuation in the appropriate places and derive rules. Discuss results. Note: Students might chart the following:
    punctuation inside quotes: . , ? !
    punctuation outside quotes: ; ? !

13. *Practice:* Students write a brief story with quotes. Note: Begin a new paragraph every time the speaker changes. Discuss and revise results in groups.

SUMMARY

Review the purpose of punctuation.

Activity

Have students load a passage from their own file disks and check for correct use of punctuation.

ADDITIONAL ACTIVITIES

1. *Literature:* A passage from the literature the class is reading can be stored on disk without punctuation. Students must insert correct punctuation.
2. *Vocabulary:* A class vocabulary list can be stored on disk. Students use list to write sentences with correct punctuation.
3. *Media:* Students write a summary of a major news story. They must write sentences and use all types of punctuation.

NOTES

Exercise for Item 2 (End marks)

1. Gilda Goose lost her head
2. Her goose is cooked
3. The family sat down for dinner

Exercise for Item 4 (Commas)

1. Roger Rita and Renee Racoon wear fur coats on a cold day.
2. Roger is a short squat racoon.
3. Rita is pretty and Renee is homely.
4. Roger who has a Masters Degree from NYU wears a silly grin.
5. In a log near the swamp Roger studies for a doctorate in animal husbandry.
6. Roger and Renee Rita told me will get married when he has his degree.

Exercise for Item 7 (Semicolons)

1. Samson and Delilah went to hairdressers' school, but they didn't last long.
2. Samson tripped on his beard, and his hair drier smashed into a mirror.
3. Delilah needed a guinea pig, but she picked the wrong one.

Exercise for Item 9 (Apostrophes)

1. The lizard of Bob is on the shoulder of Jane.
2. The book of Igor is in the hands of Charles.
3. The ribbons of the girls are in the hands of the boys.
4. Where are the hats of the women?
5. Where are the toys of the children of Mr. Jones?

6. Dont add your two cents worth.
7. Theres a sale at Lord and Taylor.

Exercise for Item 12 (Quotation marks)

1. Come over here said Farmer Brown to the turkey on Thanksgiving.
2. The turkey answered I'm chicken.
3. Outside of our door Tom said is a leopard I've just spotted.
4. Don't be silly said Joe. Leopards are born spotted.
5. Did you hear the tiger growl good men are hard to find?
6. Where's my perfume asked Sara Skunk.
7. The lamb said Bah I don't like school; Mary left him home.

MODULE 30
SENTENCE STRUCTURE

AIM

To teach students to avoid common sentence errors.

OBJECTIVES

By the end of this module, students will be able to

> Identify and correct fragments and run-ons.
> Identify and use coordinating and subordinating clauses.
> Place modifiers correctly.
> Create parallel structure.
> Identify and correct shifts in person and tense.

MATERIALS

> Exercise stored on disk. See Notes.

MOTIVATION

Load exercise stored on disk. Students read sentences to find errors.

PROCEDURE

1. Discuss sentence fragments and run-on sentences. Have students correct the errors and discuss.
2. *Exercise:* Load sentences from disk. Students edit to correct and discuss and revise with partner.
3. Ask how ideas are related in sentences.
   A. Coordinate (equal) ideas
   B. Subordinate (unequal) ideas
4. *Exercise:* Load sentences from disk. Students insert correct punctuation and/or connecting words and discuss and revise results with partner.
5. *Practice:* Students type their own examples of sentences with coordinate and subordinate ideas and discuss and revise results with partner.
6. Sometimes we put modifiers in the wrong place and as a result the meaning of the sentence is unclear. Load exercise from disk. Students should move modifiers and insert corrections and discuss and revise results with partner.
7. *Practice:* Students create sentences that contain modifiers and discuss and revise results with partner.
8. Sentences also have to have parallel structure. Load the exercise from disk. Students should correct the errors and discuss parallel structure and discuss and revise results with partner.
9. *Practice:* Students type sentences that have parallel structure and discuss and revise sentences with partner.
10. Besides avoiding unparallel sttructure, we must also avoid shifts in person and tense (in individual sentences and in paragraphs and compositions). Load exercise from disk. Students should correct shift errors and discuss and revise results with partner.
11. *Practice:* Students create their own examples of sentences that avoid shifts in person and tense and discuss and revise results with partner.

SUMMARY

Review pitfalls we should avoid in our writing.

Activity

Have students load a passage from their own file disks and check for correct sentence structure.

ADDITIONAL APPLICATIONS

1. *Literature:* Students read selections from class literature and note how professional writers avoid sentence-structure pitfalls.
2. *Vocabulary:* Class vocabulary can be stored on disk. Students create sentences using correct forms of sentence structure and avoid the errors discussed.
3. *Media:* Students combine information in two news articles on the same topic. Their sentences must demonstrate how to avoid the pitfalls discussed.

NOTES

Motivation exercise (SF, RO)

1. Henry an overweight hippo.
2. Sings in the shower.
3. Larry Lemming raced to the ocean, he carried *The New York Times* with him.

Exercise for Item 2 (SF, RO)

1. At the school door I saw a porcupine. Waiting for the bell to ring.
2. A student opened the door. Which allowed the porcupine to enter.
3. The admission of certain animals into schools is a new concept many people believe that some creatures have much intelligence but are mute.

Exercise for Item 4 (Coordinating and subordinating clauses)

1. Percy Porcupine took computer science he had difficulty with the keyboard.
2. The school supplied a voice-activated computer Percy did very well in the course.

Exercise for Item 6 (Misplaced modifiers)

1. When he saw a science student the porcupine ran out of the building holding a scalpel for a dissection.
2. Percy lost the hat from his head which was obviously not tied on properly.
3. Walking away from the school the decision may have been the wrong one thought Percy.

Exercise for Item 8 (Parallel structure)

1. Goldy Fish likes to eat, to sleep, and playing.
2. Water skiing doesn't interest Goldy as much as to go scuba diving.

3. Goldy's sister Gerty likes either basking in the sunlight or to rest quietly in the shade.

Exercise for Item 10 (Shifts in person and tense)

1. Chickens should be careful when they cross the road so that you can avoid being hit by a car.
2. Chuck Chicken looked both ways before crossing, but no cars were seen.

Index

PE
1404
.S65
1986

Solomon, Gwen
Teaching
writing with

DEC 2 1 198   DATE DUE

PE
1404
.S65
1986

Solomon, Gwen
Teaching
writing with

DATE DUE	BORROWER'S NAME
DEC 2 1 1989	*Mandan Walder*